Historical Sites

台 北 市 古 蹟 巡 覽 上冊

in Taipei I

台北市133歲古蹟中英文簡介

The Most Updated Directory
of 133 Historical Sites in Taipei

Beitou
北投區

Shilin
士林區

Zhongshan
中山區

Neihu
內湖區

Datong
大同區

Songshan
松山區

Zhongzheng
中正區

Xinyi
信義區

Nangang
南港區

Wanhua
萬華區

Daan
大安區

Wenshan
文山區

Curator : Department of Cultural Affairs,Taipei City Government
Artist Publishing Co.
策劃 / 台北市文化局 、 藝術家 出版社

Editor : Artist Publishing Co.
編輯出版 / 藝術家 出版社

Relating the Story of Taipei City to the Distant Land

City is a gigantic memory bank in which local life experiences interlace and interact with one another. As time goes by, this continual movement forms an emotional gravity for the city situated between the center and the local, which further converges with those of the other cities into a spiritual tie among their residents.

Every historical site of the city is imbued with historical depth. It was once, or still is, the field in which these experiences act upon one another. It may be a public place of worship, work, or education, or a private place of residence, business, or storage; it may be a memorial gate, a relic, a cave, a pass which harks back to the past, or a renovated factory or mansion which assumes a new appearance. These sites and buildings that stride across the public and the private, the old and the new, emit the pulse and rhythm of the everyday life of the common people, as well as their vicissitudes resulted from the changes of material life. The emotions which they generate in the collective mind are the basis on which the spiritual tie establishes itself.

Taipei City has had 133 sites which harbor a wealth of memories of everyday life, and are capable of revealing the cultural pulse of the city in its full complexity. In *Historical Sites in Taipei I* and *II*, the 2007 publication project of the Taipei City Department of Cultural Affairs and Astist Publishing Co. we attempt to identity, excavate, and explore the origin of the pulse through the memories embedded in each of the historical sites, and thereby narrate a story which belongs specifically to the residents of Taipei as the starting point to pass on the cultural force of the city. Hopefully, this effort will be carried further by the English translation of the story.

Director of the Taipei City Department of Cultural Affairs

Yongping Lee

序 言
將台北的古蹟故事，傳向遠方

城市是一個龐大的記憶體。在其中，人們的生活經驗彼此交雜作用，隨著時間的推移與沉澱，逐漸攢聚成一股情感重力，與其他城市匯流為一股緊密結合彼此的精神力量。

城市的每一處古蹟都隱含著歷史的厚度。它們曾經或至今仍為人們生活經驗的活動所在地。它們包括了公開的祭祀場所、辦公地點、教學機構和私人的樓閣住宅、營業處所、倉庫設施；包括了遙望過去的牌坊遺址、洞窟關塞和煥然更新的舊廠改建、府邸翻修。這些公私俱有、橫跨古今的古蹟建築，訴說著一般市民生活的故事，和它們隨著物質生活型態的改變而產生的時代變遷，而它們所形成的集體情感與記憶，即是那股將置身其中的人們結合起來的力量之所在。

台北市目前已擁有133處蘊涵著豐富生活記憶的古蹟，得以充分彰顯出台北城市的文化脈動。2007年初，台北市文化局與藝術家出版社合作出版《台北市古蹟巡覽》，在這分為上下兩本的手冊裡，我們一方面希望能夠透過這些古蹟的個別記憶，去辨認、發掘與細究這股脈動的源頭，記下一個特屬於台北市居民的城市故事，讓它作為傳頌台北城市文化的起點；另一方面，透過本書的中英文對照，我們也希望經由語言的羽翼，將台北城市的文化底蘊傳向遠方。

台北市文化局局長

李永萍

Historical Sites in Taipei I
台 北 市 古 蹟 巡 覽 上冊 Contents 目次

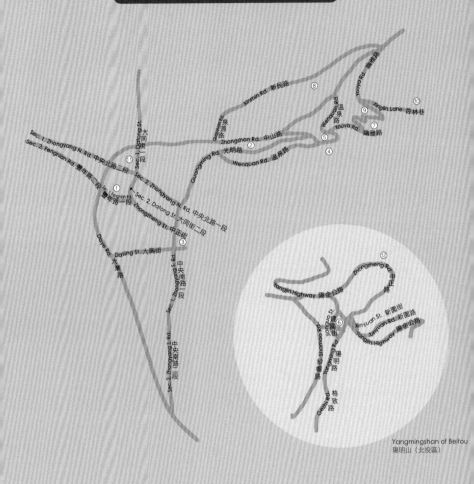

Yangmingshan of Beitou
陽明山（北投區）

① Zhou Family Widow's Memorial （周氏節孝坊）
② Beitou Hot Spring Public Bath （北投溫泉浴場）
③ Beitou Presbyterian Church （長老教會北投教室）
④ Puji Temple of Beitou （北投普濟寺）
⑤ Old Taiwan Bank Dormitory （北投台灣銀行舊宿舍）
⑥ Grass Mountain Teachers' Training Center （草山教師研習中心）
⑦ Yinsong Pavilion （吟松閣）
⑧ Former Japanese Military Hospital, Beitou Branch （前日軍衛戍醫院北投分院）
⑨ Taiwan Folk Arts Museum （北投文物館）
⑩ Beitou Grotto for the Buddhist Deity Acala （北投不動明王石窟）
⑪ The Beitou Granary （北投穀倉）
⑫ The Zhong Shan Building, Yangmingshan （陽明山中山樓）

Beitou （行政區 / 台北市北投區）

1. Zhou Family Widow's Memorial　周氏節孝坊

Completion Year / 1861
創建年代 / 清咸豐十一年

Class / 3　　　　**Category** / Memorial Gate
級別 / 第三級　　　類別 / 牌坊

Address / In front of No.36, Sec. 1, Fengnian Rd.,
Beitou District, Taipei City 112
地址 / 台北市北投區豐年路一段36號前

After the early death of her husband, Lady Zhou Juan (1788-1846) became well regarded for preserving her chastity, raising her children devotedly and remaining filial to her parents-in-law. In 1850, Governor General of Fujian and Zhejiang Liu Ke commissioned a gate to be built by the Ministry of Rites and Education in commemoration of Lady Zhou's exemplary life. Originally built of stone with four columns, three lateral sections and three levels, it was completed in 1861. Parts of the first and second levels collapsed during an earthquake in 1897. It was recently renovated by the Taipei City Government in 1992, and has become an important local landmark.

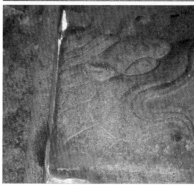

Engravings on the memorial gate（周氏節孝坊上的雕刻）

A general view of Zhou Family Widow's Memorial（周氏節孝坊全貌）

　　周氏名絹，生於清乾隆五十三年（1788），卒於道光二十六年（1846）。早年喪夫守節撫孤，侍奉翁姑至孝，其堅貞事蹟令當時任內閣中書的陳維英將建坊案呈請禮部，經禮部職名閩浙總督劉珂等於道光三十年（1850）題准建坊，坊成於咸豐十一年（1861）。此坊原爲四柱三間三層石造，光緒二十三年（1897）大地震，坊自二層以下部分倒塌，民國八十一年由市政府予以復原整修，現已成爲當地街巷之重要地標。

2. Beitou Hot Spring Public Bath (Now Beitou Hot Spring Museum)
北投溫泉浴場（今北投溫泉博物館）

Completion Year / 1913
創建年代 / 日大正二年

Class / 3
級別 / 第三級

Category / Other
類別 / 其他

Address / No.2, Zhongshan Rd., Beitou District, Taipei City 112
地址 / 台北市北投區中山路2號

Tel / 02-2893-9981

The Beitou Hot Spring Public Bath was built and opened during the early days of Japanese colonial rule, as the Japanese traditionally believed hot springs to possess healthful and therapeutic effects, yet most bathhouses at the time were too expensive for average people to afford. The Taipei Prefectural Government began constructing the Beitou Hot Spring Public Bath in 1911, and upon its completion in 1913, opened it to ordinary members of the Japanese public at reasonable rates.

The building was constructed of both bricks and wood. The first floor utilized brick-and-concrete composite walls, in the upper portion of which were placed stained glass windows, while the second floor featured wooden clapboard siding. Vents were installed in the black tile roof. The elegant building reminiscent of a British countryside villa fits perfectly with its surroundings in Beitou Park.

Through the efforts of local community members, it was declared a Class Three National Historical Site in 1997. Following renovations in 1998, the Taipei City Government transformed it into the Beitou Hot Springs Museum, introducing the building's graceful architectural elements, general knowledge of hot springs, and the unique characteristics of hot spring baths in Taiwan.

The current state of Beitou Hot Spring Museum（現今北投溫泉博物館外觀一景）

The current state of the old bathtub（舊浴池現貌 *）

The entrance to Beitou Hot
Spring Museum
（北投溫泉博物館入口＊）

　　北投溫泉開發利用於日治初期，因日人傳統上認為溫泉具有養身與復健的功效，惟當時提供泡湯場所多為高消費之溫泉旅館，非一般人所能負擔。1911年台北州廳動工興建公共浴場，1913年落成啓用，名為「北投溫泉浴場」，提供來自日本本土的一般民眾平價使用。

　　建築的構造由磚木混築，一樓採清水紅磚砌牆，上開彩繪玻璃窗，二樓採木構造外覆雨淋板，黑瓦屋頂為了透氣而設有通風窗，整座建築外觀頗具英國鄉間別墅風貌，外觀典雅，並與北投公園融為一體。

　　1997年經地方人士的努力，成為三級古蹟，後經市政府於隔年進行修復及再利用規劃，作為北投溫泉博物館使用，運用溫泉建築之特色，介紹台灣特有的溫泉浴池，並以展示及解說提供溫泉相關知識。

The distinctive glass painting on the arch-shaped window
（館內的弧形窗上鑲嵌的玻璃畫很有特色＊）

3. Beitou Presbyterian Church 長老教會北投教堂

Completion Year / 1912
創建年代 / 日大正元年

Class / Municipal
級別 / 市定

Category / Church
類別 / 教堂

Address / No.77, Sec. 1, Zhongyang S. Rd., Beitou District, Taipei City 112
地址 / 台北市北投區中央南路一段77號

Tel / 02-2891-2370

The Beitou Presbyterian Church was established by Canadian missionary George Leslie Mackay. One of the oldest church buildings in Taipei, it was designed by Canadian missionary William Gauld in 1912. Originally, the congregation was made up mostly of plains aborigines from the Beitou area. The building serves as valuable historical evidence of Western religious development in Taiwan. Constructed of red bricks with a wooden frame in a style similar to British country churches, the exterior walls were reinforced with buttresses to protect against earthquakes. It is also highly significant as the only surviving church designed by William Gauld in the 20th century.

The interior of Beitou Presbyterian Church
（長老教會北投教堂內部）

Above : The main entrance to Beitou Presbyterian Church（上圖：長老教會北投教堂正面入口）

Below : Pillars are combined with the outer wall of the church to prevent shock（下圖：長老教會北投教堂外牆設有扶壁柱，具抗震作用。）

北投教會爲加拿大傳教士馬偕所創，台灣北部基督長老教會所建的教堂，也是台北附近僅存的古老教堂之一，由加拿大來台的傳教士吳威廉（William Gauld）於1912年所設計建造。當時附近信徒多爲北投的平埔族人，在台灣近代宗教發展史上具有見證之價值。教堂以紅磚及木屋架構成，風格接近英式鄉村教堂，外牆使用加強耐震的扶壁，本教堂爲20世紀由吳威廉所設計的教堂中現今僅存的孤例，值得保存。

4. Puji Temple of Beitou　北投普濟寺

Completion Year / 1905
創建年代 / 日明治三十八年

Class / Municipal
級別 / 市定

Category / Temple
類別 / 祠廟

Address / No.122, Wenquan Rd., Beitou District, Taipei City 112
地址 / 台北市北投區溫泉路112號

Tel / 02-2891-4386

Puji Temple of Beitou is a rare example of a temple of the Shingon sect of Japanese Vajrayana Buddhism to be founded in Taiwan. Originally named Tiezhen Temple, it was first built in 1905 from donations by Japanese railway employees. It is dedicated to the Goddess of Mercy Avalokiteshvara, who serves as a guardian spirit of hot springs. Constructed in a Japanese style, its framework is well preserved. The main hall has a single-eaved gable-and-hip roof. Its floor plan is almost perfectly square, with both a width and a depth of three *kaijian*

The entrance to Puji Temple of Beitou
（普濟寺入口外觀）

(a Kaijian traditional unit of measurement equivalent to the standard width of a single room). The roof stretches forward, forming a cover for the front entrance – a popular design feature during the Edo Period in Japan. The entire temple is built of high-quality juniper. The wooden brackets and curved tie beams are decorated with elegant carvings. Of particular note are the bell-shaped windows. The main hall, the stone Avalokiteshvara image and the stele dedicated to Taiwan Railway Administration director Murakami Shoichi are all of great historical value.

A typical Japanese-style building, the temple has an aura of tranquility and elegance. （本寺為典型的日式建築，具清靜優雅之韻味。）

北投普濟寺爲台灣罕見的日本眞言宗佛寺，1905年由日籍鐵道部員工集資興建，原名鐵眞寺。寺中供奉湯守觀音，佛寺採用日式風格，平面佈局保存極爲完整，在台灣並不多見。大殿建築爲單簷的歇山式，面寬三開間，進深亦得三間，近正方形，屋頂向前伸出，成爲入口玄關，爲日本江戶時期常用的形式。全殿以高級檜木建造，斗拱及虹樑雕刻精美，鐘形窗子亦具特色。除大殿外，湯守觀音石佛像與村上彰一翁碑等文物同樣深具價值。

The interior of Puji Temple of Beitou （普濟寺內景）

5. Old Taiwan Bank Dormitory　北投台灣銀行舊宿舍

Completion Year / around 1920
創建年代 / 日大正年間

Class / Municipal
級別 / 市定

Category / Residence
類別 / 宅第

Address / No.103, Wenquan Rd., Beitou District, Taipei City 112
地址 / 台北市北投區溫泉路103號

The Old Taiwan Bank Dormitory in Beitou is formed of three main buildings and a courtyard. The first building, situated closest to the road, was built around 1935, and originally served as the Shin Matsushita Hotel. The other two buildings, built circa 1922 as the private villas of businessman Kozuka Kaneyoshi, were later purchased by Shin Matsushita and incorporated into the hotel grounds.

Around 1941, the Taiwan Bank purchased the Shin Matsushita Hotel, using it as a club and lodge. Following World War II, it was converted to a dormitory for employees of the Bank of Taiwan and their families. The whole building is shaped similar to a bridge and traverses a streambed, blending harmoniously with its natural surroundings, and serving as a recreational venue of superlative quality. The building is highly valuable for its rare combination of Japanese exterior and Western decorative features.

北投台灣銀行舊宿舍是由三棟主體建築和庭園組成。最接近道路的第一棟約興建於1935年，原為新松島旅館。其餘二棟是商人小塚兼吉的別墅，大約興建於1922年，後為新松島收購，成為旅館的一部分。

This building combines Japanese and Western architectural features. The bowery pertruding from the building is the entrance to the dormitory. (此建築物為和洋混合風格，前凸出小亭為入口玄關)

1941年左右，台灣銀行收購新松島旅館，作爲俱樂部及宿舍。光復以後，則改爲台灣銀行眷屬宿舍，整座建築有如一座橋樑，橫跨於溪谷之上，配合地形將建築物融入自然風景中，是一處絕佳的休憩場所。這座建築融合日式外觀及洋式建築裝飾，形成罕見的「和洋混合」風格，極具保存價值。

The Western-style back building has pillars on which sophiscated decorations are applied. (後棟建築屬於西式建築式樣，柱頭有精美裝飾)

6. Grass Mountain Teachers' Training Center
(Taipei Teachers' In-Service Education Center)

草山教師研習中心（台北市教師研習中心）

Completion Year / 1929
創建年代 / 日昭和四年

Class / Municipal
級別 / 市定

Category / Other
類別 / 其他

Address / No.2, Jianguo St., Beitou District, Taipei City 112
地址 / 台北市北投區陽明山建國街2號

Tel / 02-2861-6942

Originally known as the Grass Mountain Public Recreational Garden, this historical building was the most renowned public bathhouse in the Yangmingshan area when it was first built. At the time, the hot springs of Grass Mountain attracted visitors from near and far, and these facilities were constructed on a very large scale, divided into two bathing pools, for men and women, respectively. Its most distinguishing feature is the octagonal bathing pool. After World War II, the bathhouse became an office building for the Yangmingshan Administration Bureau. Today it serves as a teachers' in-service training center of the Taipei city Bureau of Education. The building was constructed from locally obtained materials. The walls were built of blocks of andesite, the purple-gray tint of which matches the tiles of the building's slanted roofs. Well-known craftsmen from Danshui constructed the building. The arrangement of the stone blocks was influenced by Western architecture, and thus the bathhouse was originally renowned for its "oreign design." It stands as valuable evidence of the history of Taiwan's hot spring culture, and its application of building materials and architectural techniques.

The current appearance of Taipei Teachers' In-Service Education Center(今台北市教師研習中心外觀一景＊)

　　原名草山眾樂園，完工後成為草山最著名的公共浴場。草山溫泉遠近馳名，當時建造這座規模宏大的公共澡堂，內分男女浴池，其八角形浴池最具特色。戰後公共浴場改為陽明山管理局辦公廳舍，現為台北市教師研習中心。建築的設計係就地取材而成，運用草山附近盛產的安山岩砌築牆體，紫灰色色調配上斜頂屋瓦，由當時淡水名匠施工，石塊排列受西洋建築影響，被稱為「番仔砥」。本浴場在台灣溫泉文化史與建材運用技巧方面皆有重要價值。

The stone walls of the building, which are bricked with the Western techniques, are characterized by irregular grey lining. (建物石牆用西式砌法，以灰縫線錯開是其特色。＊)

7. Yinsong Pavilion　吟松閣

Completion Year / 1934
創建年代 / 日昭和九年

Class / Municipal
級別 / 市定

Category / Other
類別 / 其他

Address / No.21, Youya Rd., Beitou District, Taipei City 112
地址 / 台北市北投區幽雅路21號

Tel / 02-2895-1531

Located in the Beitou hot spring district, Yinsong Pavilion, constructed in 1934, is one of a handful of Japanese-style wooden hotels still remaining in Taipei. Its architecture and the landscaping of its inner courtyard are of classic Japanese design. It is a mainly single-story structure, with a two-story section, and is covered with black roof tiles. The appearance is peaceful and classically elegant. Although it has undergone restoration several times, it retains its original wooden entry room, fishpond, small arched bridge, stone stairs and stone lanterns, reflecting the style of courtyard design in the Taisho and Showa periods. Laid out along a mountain slope, the whole building affords an excellent view. The interior is furbished with a large amount of Formosan juniper, creating a luxurious and charming atmosphere. With its classic architectural and garden design, Yinsong Pavilion stands as a testimony to the cultural history of the Beitou hot spring district.

The Japanese-style courtyard of Yingsong Pavilion（吟松閣的日式庭院＊）

Yinsong Pavilion is one of the historical hot spring hotels in Beitou. (吟松閣是北投的古蹟溫泉旅館＊)

The interior of Yingsong Pavilion（吟松閣室內一景＊）

位於北投溫泉地帶的吟松閣建於1934年，為目前台北附近所存的少數日本式木造旅館，其建築物及庭園造景深具日式風格之代表性，主體建築多為鋪黑瓦平房，部分為二層樓，外觀極為幽靜而典雅。內部歷經多次整建，惟仍保留屋前入口木門樓、魚池、小拱橋、石階與石燈籠，充分反映了日本大正與昭和年間的庭園設計風格。整座旅館利用地形，沿山坡配置，視野良好，室內運用大量檜木裝修，呈現高貴優雅之氣氛，從建築風格與庭園佈置而言，吟松閣見證了北投溫泉文化史。

8. Former Japanese Military Hospital, Beitou Branch
(Now Beitou Armed Forces Hospital)
前日軍衛戍醫院北投分院（今國軍北投醫院）

Completion Year / around 1910
創建年代 / 約日大正初年

Class / Municipal
級別 / 市定

Category / Other
類別 / 其他

Address / No.60, Xinmin Rd., Beitou District, Taipei City 112
地址 / 台北市北投區新民路60號

Tel / 02-2895-9808

Built during the Japanese colonial period (1895-1945), the Beitou branch of the Japanese Military Hospital serviced wounded Japanese soldiers convalescing here during the Russo-Japanese War. It later became a psychiatric hospital for the ROC Armed Forces. Several buildings were arranged side-by-side in rows across a mountain slope. One entranceway is currently extant. The buildings were constructed with relatively tall foundations, and were positioned facing south, with corridors along both sides, serving to block both moisture and sunlight. Built in a typical architectural style of that time, both the walls and framework were of wood, with clapboard sidings and small wooden windows. The buildings are notable for their incorporation of native Taiwanese materials.

日治時期爲日軍衛戍醫院北投分院，提供日俄戰爭中之傷兵療養，戰後成爲國軍精神病患醫院。建築物順著山坡等高線配置，前後數列並排，今保存入口一座。建築物有較高的台基，坐北朝南且兩面設置迴廊，具防潮防曬功效。牆體及屋架爲木結構，牆壁採用雨淋板及木板小窗，爲當時典型作法。建築以融合台灣鄉土材料爲其特色。

Doorway to the front building of the Former Japanese Military Hospital, Beitou Branch（前日軍衛戍醫院北投分院前棟入口門廊）

The corridors of the Former Japanese Military Hospital, Beitou Branch（前日軍衛戍醫院北投分院迴廊景色）

9. Taiwan Folk Arts Museum　北投文物館

- **Completion Year** / around 1925
  創建年代 / 日大正十四年前後

- **Class** / Municipal　　　**Category** / Other
  級別 / 市定　　　　　　**類別** / 其他

- **Address** / No.32, Youya Rd., Beitou District, Taipei City 112
  地址 / 台北市北投區幽雅路32號

- **Tel** / 02-2891-2318

In the early Japanese colonial period (1895-1945), Beitou became famous for its hot springs, and gradually developed into a holiday and health resort. This completely wooden villa first served as a Japanese officer's club, and for a time housed a kamikaze air squadron. After World War II, the Ministry of Foreign Affairs converted it into the Jia Shan Guest House, and later sold it to private buyers. In recent years, it has been converted into the Taiwan Folk Arts Museum. The complex is divided into a higher and a lower group of buildings, all made of wood in a Japanese style. The main building has two stories, with a large hall on the second floor, exquisitely hand-crafted of quality wood. The Japanese-style garden that is part of the teahouse also remains in perfect condition, with a small bridge crossing a flowing stream, an artificial hill and a waterfall.

The entrance to the Taiwan Folk Arts Museum before it was renovated（整修前的北投文物館入口外觀）

The elegant Japanese-style garden（優美的日式庭院造景＊）

北投因有溫泉之勝，日治初期逐漸成為休假或療養性質的地區。這座純木造別莊初作為日本軍官俱樂部，一度曾為神風特攻隊所使用。戰後被利用為外交部的佳山招待所，後再轉賣民間，近年改為北投文物館。建築分為高低兩群，皆為日式木造建物，特別是主體房舍為二樓式，樓上有精緻大廳，木材及手工皆精。茶藝館附屬的日式庭園亦完整，有小橋流水及假山飛瀑之勝景。

The interior of the Taiwan Folk Arts Museum（北投文物館內景）

Above Left: A view of the refurbished Taiwan Folk Arts Musuem
（整修過的北投文物館建物一角＊）（左頁上圖）
Below Left: Tao-Ren Ju in the Taiwan Folk Arts Museum
（北投文物館內陶然居）（左頁下圖）

10. Beitou Grotto for the Buddhist Deity Acala
北投不動明王石窟

Completion Year / 1925
創建年代 / 日大正十四年

Class / Municipal
級別 / 市定

Category / Other
類別 / 其他

Address / Across from No.2, Xinglin Lane, Youya Rd., Beitou District, Taipei City 112
地址 / 台北市北投區幽雅路杏林巷2號對面

The Acala Grotto is a rare example of a Buddhist grotto in Taiwan. Acala is one of the Five Wisdom Kings of Vajrayana, or Tantric Buddhism. A guardian deity generally portrayed with a fearsome appearance, Acala is also held to be an embodiment of the Buddha. Acala (Fudo in Japanese) is commonly venerated by the Shingon sect of Buddhism in Japan, but rarely seen in Taiwan. Japanese businessman Sano Sotaro established the grotto in 1925 in conjunction with his hot spring hotel, chiseling the small cave in the rock, and placing in it a small idol of Acala. With a hand-washing basin in front and a clear-spring waterfall at the side of the grotto, it is a tranquil and elegant locale.

The stone Buddhist statues in the Acala Grotto
（北投不動明王石窟中石雕神像）

A front view of the Acala Grotto（北投不動明王石窟外觀）

　　不動明王石窟爲台灣較少見的佛教石窟，佛教密宗護法神有五大明王又稱五大尊，其神態多爲威猛之形，不動明王爲五大明王之一，又有謂不動明王爲大如來之化身，屬密教之眞言宗，在台灣並不多見。北投不動明王石窟爲1925年日人佐野庄太郎爲配合其所經營之溫泉旅館而倡建，其利用岩石鑿洞，內安置石雕神像，規模小巧，前有手水台，洞旁清泉飛瀑，景色幽雅。

The water bench in front of the Acala Grotto, used for handwashing and drinking（北投不動明王石窟前的水台，供淨手與飲用）

11. The Beitou Granary　北投穀倉

Completion Year / 1938
創建年代 / 日昭和十三年

Class / Municipal
級別 / 市定

Category / Other
類別 / 其他

Address / No.153, Datong St., Beitou District, Taipei City 112
地址 / 台北市北投區大同街153號

Tel / 02-2892-4185

Built in 1938 during Japanese colonial rule, the Beitou Granary was operated by the Beitou Credit and Purchasing Cooperative. Starting in 1904, the Japanese colonial government adopted grain distribution measures, in response to wartime exigencies, and controlled the entire process, from production and storage to sales. The Beitou Granary became a government-designated grain storage center. After World War II, Beitou established a farmer's association, which continued to provide farmers with services, including supplies, sales and loans. The layout of the granary was in an L shape. Facilities included offices, a mill room and a long grain storage area. A raised loft was constructed on the roof for ventilation. A conveyor belt ran down the middle of the interior, separating the granary into right and left storehouses. A corridor made of brick provided insulation. A total of 12 storage rooms were partitioned by brick walls, on which were hung woven bamboo nets to protect rice husks from moisture. The entire roof truss was made of wood, and has survived in good condition to the present day. Particularly noteworthy is the rice mill, made of high-quality juniper, which is still well preserved.

Above: The open roof of the Beitou Granary helps to dissipate heat that facilitates rice preservation. （北投穀倉太子樓屋頂可散熱，利於保存稻穀。）（上圖）

Below: The entrance to the office of the Beitou Granary which was used as Grain Laboratory （北投穀倉辦公室入口，昔為稻穀檢驗室。＊）（下圖）

The machine room of old Beitou Granary has grinding machines in the old days.
（昔日北投穀倉的機械房，內有碾米機）

　　北投穀倉建於日治時期昭和十三年（1938），當時屬於有限責任
北投信用購買組合所經營。從1904年開始，爲因應二次大戰，台灣
總督府採取糧食配給的措施，從生產、儲存到銷售全部管制，北投穀
倉成爲官方指定儲存糧食的處所。戰後，北投成立農會，繼續爲農民
服務，除了供銷外又有信用貸款之服務。北投穀倉平面呈曲尺形，包
括辦公室、碾米機房及長條形的穀倉，穀倉的屋頂凸出通氣小屋頂，
俗稱爲太子樓，內部以中央輸送帶分爲左右兩邊的倉庫，並以磚造拱
廊予以隔熱。穀倉共分隔爲十二間，隔牆以磚砌成，牆上有竹編網，
可使稻穀避潮，屋頂桁架全爲木結構，迄今仍保存完整。值得重視的
是碾米機設備爲質地優良之檜木所造，目前仍保存良好。

12. The Zhong Shan Building, Yangmingshan
陽明山中山樓

Completion Year / 1965
創建年代 / 民國五十四年

Class / Municipal
級別 / 市定

Category / Other
類別 / 其他

Address / No.15, Sec. 2, Yangming Rd.,
Beitou District, Taipei City 112
地址 / 台北市北投區陽明路2段15號

The Zhong Shan Building was constructed in 1965 to commemorate the centennial birthday of Dr. Sun Yatsen, father of the Republic of China, and the renaissance of Chinese culture. It was meticulously designed by noted architect Hsiu Tze-lan according to the personal concepts of then ROC president Chiang Kai-shek and his wife Madame Soong Mei-ling. The entire building is based on China's tradition of imperial architecture, with a cascading structure and roof of green glazed tiles. The upturned eaves convey a dramatic sense of motion, as if the unfolding of a great bird's wings. The complementary combination of red eaves and white walls makes the building appear particularly magnificent.

The archway of Zhong Shan Building is inscribed with words "Road to Righteousness" (陽明山中山樓「大道之行」牌樓＊）

The Zhong Shan Building of Yangmingshan and one of the stone lions in front of the main emtrance
（陽明山中山樓及門前石獅子＊）

The Zhong Shan Building is an important venue for state banquets, major government conferences and receptions. Its Chinese Culture Hall, the dedicated conference area for the ROC National Assembly, is of particular historical significance as a witness to the constitutional development of the Republic of China.

中山樓係民國五十四年，政府為紀念國父百年誕辰暨復興中華文化所興建，由修澤蘭建築師親聆先總統蔣公暨夫人之構想，精心設計而成。全樓以中國宮殿式建築藝術為藍本，樓之結構層層疊疊，屋頂舖以綠色琉璃瓦，飛簷翹角有如大鵬展翼，活潑而生動，搭配紅簷白牆，尤顯壯麗。

建物使用上定位為政府舉辦國宴、召開重要會議及接待國內外貴賓的重要場所，尤以樓內的「中華文化堂」為國民大會的專屬開會場所，見證我國憲政發展之歷史意義。

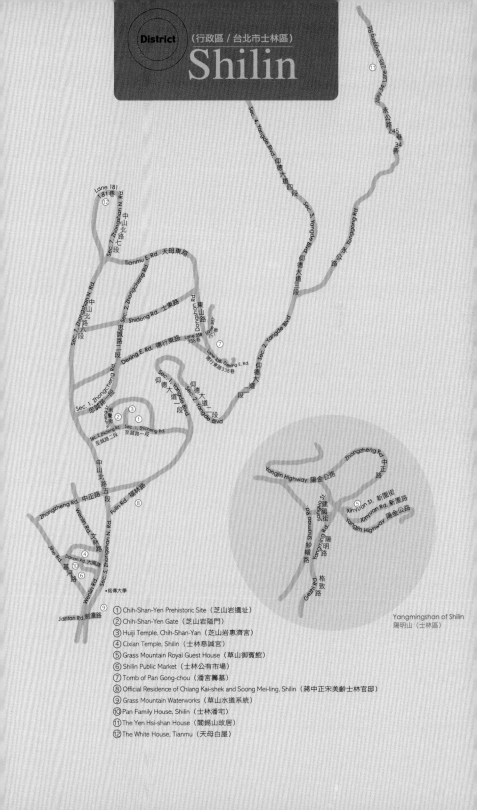

District

（行政區／台北市士林區）

Shilin

① Chih-Shan-Yen Prehistoric Site（芝山岩遺址）
② Chih-Shan-Yen Gate（芝山岩隘門）
③ Huiji Temple, Chih-Shan-Yan（芝山岩惠濟宮）
④ Cixian Temple, Shilin（士林慈諴宮）
⑤ Grass Mountain Royal Guest House（草山御賓館）
⑥ Shilin Public Market（士林公有市場）
⑦ Tomb of Pan Gong-chou（潘宮籌墓）
⑧ Official Residence of Chiang Kai-shek and Soong Mei-ling, Shilin（蔣中正宋美齡士林官邸）
⑨ Grass Mountain Waterworks（草山水道系統）
⑩ Pan Family House, Shilin（士林潘宅）
⑪ The Yen Hsi-shan House（閻錫山故居）
⑫ The White House, Tianmu（天母白屋）

Yangmingshan of Shilin
陽明山（士林區）

Shilin （行政區 / 台北市士林區）

1. Chih-Shan-Yen Prehistoric Site　芝山岩遺址

Completion Year / 3000 to 4000 years ago
創建年代 / 約4000~3000年前

Class / 2　　　　**Category** / Historic Site
級別 / 第二級　　　**類別** / 遺址

Address / Atop Chi-Shan-Yen., Shilin District, Taipei City 111
地址 / 台北市士林區芝山岩小山

In ancient times, Chih-Shan-Yen was an islet in the lake that filled Taipei basin. During the Japanese colonial period （1895-1945）, archaeological remains were found at Chih-Shan-Yen, making it the first archaeological site in Taiwan. Archaeological research has revealed remains from two prehistoric cultures – the Chih-Shan-Yen culture and the Yuanshan culture. The remains of the Yuanshan culture can be seen on the side slopes and the top of Chih-Shan-Yen, and along the sides of Zhicheng Road and Yusheng Road. Archaeological remains from the Chih-Shan-Yen culture can only be seen in between Yu Nong Elementary School and the Stone Deity Shrine in the northwest corner of Chih-Shan-Yen. Compared to other prehistoric cultures of Taiwan, the Chih-Shan-Yen culture has yielded a rich variety of excavated cultural artifacts, including ceramic, stone, bone and shell products, as well as rice, woven grass, wooden utensils and other objects indicative of an advanced culture.

芝山岩在遠古時期是台北盆地湖泊中之一小島，日治時期由日人發現，是台灣考古史上第一個被發現的遺址。據考古研究顯示，它主要保存著兩層史前文化，即芝山岩文化與圓山文化。圓山文化遺址的分佈範圍較廣，在芝山岩山頂、山坡與至誠路及雨聲路環山道路兩側均可見之，而芝山岩文化遺址分佈的

Above: The interior of the exhibition hall of archaeological excavation（芝山岩文化史蹟公園中的考古探坑展示館內一景＊）（上圖）

Right: The exhibition hall of archaeological excavation in the Park of Chih-Shan-Yen Prehistoric Site（芝山岩文化史蹟公園中的考古探坑展示館＊）（中圖）

Below: A bird's eye view of the Chih-Shan-Yen Prehistoric Site（芝山岩遺址鳥瞰）（下圖）

範圍僅見於西北角的石頭公廟與雨農國小之間。芝山岩文化在台灣所發現的史前文化中，出土文物內容非常豐富，除了陶、石、骨、貝器之外，並發現有稻米、草編、木器等進步的遺存物。

2. Chih-Shan-Yen Gate　芝山岩隘門

Completion Year / 1825
創建年代 / 清道光五年

Class / 3
級別 / 第三級

Category / Pass
類別 / 關塞

Address / The west side of Huiji Temple, Shilin District, Taipei City 111
地址 / 台北市士林區惠濟宮西側

Built in 1825, Chih-Shan-Yen Gate is a remnant of armed conflict between two communities of immigrants from Zhangzhou and Quanzhou (both in Fujian Province). Made of locally quarried stones, the gate was a defensive construction of the people from Zhangzhou. The top of the wall was crenellated, with loopholes through which weapons could be fired. The original fortification included four gates, positioned east, west, north and south, of which only the west gate is extant. Inside the gate can be found Huiji Temple and a funerary temple. On the rock outside the gate are four Chinese characters inscribed by noted Qing-dynasty scholar Pan Yongqing, depicting the enchanted beauty of Chih-Shan-Yen.

　　芝山岩隘門，建於清道光五年（1825），為漳泉械鬥之遺跡，此門係昔日漳州人之防禦工事，以當地所產石材構築，石城上設雉堞、銃孔。原門有四座，並以東、西、南、北名之，今存者僅有西門。門內有惠濟宮、大墓公諸聖蹟，門外巨岩上刻有「洞天福地」四大字，為清代士林名士潘永清所題，闡明芝山岩富有鍾靈毓秀之美。

Right: The Chih-Shan-Yan Gate is bricked with stones.（芝山岩隘門以石塊砌成＊）（上圖）

Below: A view from inside the Chih-Shan-Yan Gate（芝山岩隘門內一景＊）（下圖）

3. Huiji Temple, Chih-Shan-Yan　芝山岩惠濟宮

Completion Year / 1752
創建年代 / 清乾隆十七年

Class / 3
級別 / 第三級

Category / Temple
類別 / 祠廟

Address / No.26, Lane 326, Sec. 1, Zhicheng Rd., Shilin District, Taipei City 111
地址 / 台北市士林區至誠路一段326巷26號

Tel / 02-2831-1728

Built between 1752 and 1764, Huiji Temple is dedicated to the worship of the Sage King Chen Yuanguang, founder of the Zhangzhou district of Fujian. The temple has been rebuilt five times. The current structure was constructed in 1968. It is made predominantly of cement, in which a few stone sculptures from older generations of the temple have been inlaid. The front hall is dedicated to the Sage King Chen Yuanguang, while the upper floor of the rear hall is dedicated to the god of scholarship Wen Chang, and the lower hall is dedicated to the Buddhist deity Avalokiteshvara.

In 1786, rebel military leader Lin Shuangwen rose up against the Qing authorities, attacking Zhishan. In the Lin Shuangwen Incident, many local people of Shilin were massacred next to Huiji Temple. A tablet was later erected at this location as a memorial. Other architectural remnants from the early period of settlement in Shilin, such as the Zhishan Huaigu Pavilion, a tablet attesting to the donation of the grounds, a narrow gate originally part of fortifications, and a funerary temple, can still be found in the vicinity.

Above: The archway in front of Huiji Temple（惠濟宮外的牌樓＊）（上圖）

Right: The statue of Saintly Emperor Guan in Huiji Temple（惠濟宮內的關聖帝君像＊）（下圖）

Huiji Temple has a manificent outlook that assumes the features of Minnan temples. （惠濟宮外觀壯麗，具閩南式廟宇的風貌。＊）

　　芝山岩惠濟宮，奉祀開漳聖王陳元光，廟始建於清乾隆十七年（1752），於二十九年（1764）竣工，其後歷經五次重建，今廟係民國57年重建結果，結構多為水泥構造，僅局部嵌入舊有石雕。前殿主祀開漳聖王，後殿樓上配祀文昌帝君，樓下祀觀音菩薩。

　　清乾隆五十一年（1786）林爽文事變，林爽文部將率軍攻打芝山，士林地方人士將之盡殲於廟旁，廟旁立有「惠濟宮碑誌」記載其事，附近尚有懷古亭、芝山合約碑記、隘門、同歸所等，留存士林開闢初期遺蹟。

4. Cixian Temple, Shilin　士林慈誠宮

Completion Year / 1796 **創建年代** / 清嘉慶元年	
Class / 3 **級別** / 第三級	**Category** / Temple **類別** / 祠廟
Address / No.84, Danan Rd., Shilin District, Taipei City 111 **地址** / 台北市士林區大南路84號	
Tel / 02-2881-1083	

Cixian Temple, dedicated to the worship of the goddess Mazu, was originally built in 1796 near the current location of the American School in Shilin. In 1864, a group of devotees including Pan Yongqing and Pan Shengqing built a new temple on New Bazhilan Street, to provide a guardian deity for the area. The temple was rebuilt in 1927. Artisans of two different schools separately constructed the left and right sides, which consequently contain different styles of carvings. The exquisite koji ceramic art in the main hall is also a significant feature.

The interior of Cixian Temple
（慈誠宮內一景）

A general view of Cixian Temple, Shilin（士林慈諴宮外貌＊）（上圖）
Details of the gourd-shaped roof truss in the main hall of Cixan Temple
（士林慈諴宮正殿瓜型的屋架細部）（下圖）

　　士林慈諴宮，奉祀天上聖母，創建於清嘉慶元年（1796），原址在今士林美國學校附近。清同治三年（1864），由善信潘永清、潘盛清等，遷建於八芝蘭新街，爲該街守護神。民國十六年重建時，左右兩邊由兩派匠師分別承建，故雕琢作風各異，正殿內仍有精美的交趾陶，皆具重要特色。

5. Grass Mountain Royal Guest House　草山御賓館

Completion Year / 1923
創建年代 / 日大正十二年

Class / Municipal
級別 / 市定

Category / Residence
類別 / 宅第

Address / No.1, Xinyuan St., Shilin District, Taipei City 111
地址 / 台北市士林區新園街1號

"Grass Mountain" was an old name for the Yangmingshan area. During the era of Japanese colonial rule, it became a newly developed recreational district, due to its excellent hot springs and superlative mountain scenery. In April of 1923, Japan's Crown Prince Hirohito toured Taiwan, and the colonial administration selected Grass Mountain as one of the points his entourage would visit. They built the Grass Mountain Royal Guest House as his personal lodgings. Located in a mountain valley, the building is secluded and quiet. Its architectural style is a unique mixture of Japanese and Western influences.

After World War II, Grass Mountain Royal Guest House became known as Yangmingshan First Guest House, and hosted confidential meetings of the Chinese Nationalist Party.

A signpost to the historic site of the Grass Mountain Royal Guest House（草山御賓館 的古蹟指示牌＊）

Sun Ke, president of the Examination Yuan, later lived here, and the house eventually became a residence for the descendants of ROC founding father Dr. Sun Yat-sen.

　　草山是陽明山的舊稱，日治時期因溫泉泉質甚佳且充滿山林景色，成為新興的遊憩地。大正十二年（1923）四月，日本皇太子裕仁來台視察，台灣總督府選定草山為遊覽地點之一，同時著手興建御賓館供其休憩。這棟建築位於山谷之中，環境優美且清靜，具有日本住家與西洋小住宅之混合風格，頗具特色。

　　台灣光復之後，草山御賓館改為陽明山第一賓館，提供黨政軍開機密會議使用，其後考試院院長孫科入住，此後成為國父後人在台灣的住所。

Above: The entrance to the Grass Mountain Royal Guest House （草山御賓館入口外觀）（上圖）

Below: An old photograph of the Grass Mountain Royal Guest House in the 1920s （草山御賓館在1920年代外貌的老照片）（下圖）

6. Shilin Public Market（Shilin Market）
士林公有市場（士林市場）

Completion Year / 1913
創建年代 / 日大正二年

Class / Municipal
級別 / 市定

Category / Other
類別 / 其他

Address / No.89, Danan Rd., Shilin District, Taipei City 111
地址 / 台北市士林區大南路89號

The Shilin Public Market is located in front of Cixian Temple. In the Qing dynasty, Cixian Temple, dedicated to the goddess Mazu, was situated in the center of Shilin, and the plaza in front of it held a busy market. In the early period of Japanese rule, the Japanese colonial government began exacting public health fees, used to help Japanese people purchase goods and to ensure their health. In 1896, they established the Xinqi Street Market in the Ximen area, the first of Taipei City's government-administered markets.

Later on, the Japanese initiated a city-restructuring plan, converting the plaza in front of Cixian Temple into a public market in 1913. A symbolic merger of traditional temple forecourt markets and modern public markets, it is of significant historical and folkloric value. Other public markets representative of that era, such as those in the Ximen, Dadaocheng and Nanmen districts, have for the most part been altered. Only the Shilin Public Market retains its original appearance and remains a market of considerable scale. In addition to the central building, arched shopping arcades stand on either side. Its special architectural features include tall brick walls at both ends, roof vents, numerous buttresses along the side walls, and pointed-arch windows.

The semi-circled gable and roof of Shilin Public Market
（士林公有市場的半圓形山牆及屋頂一角）（上圖）

The roof of Shilin Public Market（士林公有市場的屋頂）（下圖）

　　士林公有市場位於著名的媽祖廟慈誠宮之前，在清代士林建街時，慈誠宮位於市街中心，廟埕前即為熱鬧的市集。日治初期，日本政府為便利日人採買及保護日人之健康，遂撥出公共衛生費，於1896年興建西門町新起街市場，此為台北市公營市場之開始。

　　後來日人實施所謂都市改正計畫，士林慈誠宮廟口前闢建為公有市場並於1913年落成，象徵傳統廟口與近代公有市場之結合，具有歷史與民俗之價值。當時台北地區代表性公有市場有西門町新起街市場、大稻埕市場及南門市場等，如今大多已改建，僅士林公有市場尚保存原貌，且市場規模宏大，除了中央的大屋架建築外，左右兩側尚有拱廊式店鋪，兩端有磚砌的高大山牆，屋頂上闢有通氣窗，側牆上有許多扶壁，窗子採弧形拱，表現出諸多建築設計上的特色。

7. Tomb of Pan Gong-chou　潘宮籌墓

Completion Year / 1870
創建年代 / 清同治九年

Class / Municipal
級別 / 市定

Category / Tomb
類別 / 陵墓

Address / Lot No. 595, Sub-section No. 2, Jhihlan Section, Shilin District, Taipei City 111
地址 / 台北市士林區芝蘭段二小段595地號

Pan Gongchou was one of the first immigrants from the Zhangzhou district of China's Fujian Province to settle in the Taipei basin during the Qing dynasty. Homesteading in Shilin, he also opened up Beitou, Danshui, Shimen and Sanzhi for development. At the end of the Qing dynasty, the original town of Shilin was

A general view of the Tomb of Pan Gong-chou (士林潘宮籌墓全景)

destroyed by fire during clashes between groups of immigrants from Zhangzhou and Quanzhou. Therefore, under the leadership of the Pan family, the Zhangzhou settlers relocated to Xiashulin and laid out a new grid of streets with a temple to the goddess Mazu at its center, serving as the foundation for the current street plan of Shilin District. The tomb of Pan Gongchou was built on a mountain slope in the foothills of Shilin near the Tianmu area, in a location called Hongluxue, with excellent conditions according to the theories of Fengshui. A tombstone was erected in 1870, and remains well preserved to this day. The tomb is large, and its stone elephants and altar are still discernible. The tombstone's inscription displays verse written by scholars and officials of Taipei at that time. Recently, the descendants of Pan Gongchou founded an association responsible for maintenance of the tomb.

　　潘宮籌為清代台北盆地漳州移民之領袖人物，居於今士林一帶，其墾拓範圍廣及士林、北投、淡水、石門、三芝等地。清末因漳泉械鬥，士林舊街被焚毀，潘氏家族率領漳人移居下樹林，並以媽祖廟慈諴宮為中心規劃闢建新市街，為今天士林市街奠下基礎，貢獻頗多。潘宮籌墓位於士林近天母之山區，依山而建，俗稱烘爐穴之風水地，形勢頗佳。潘宮籌生前被封為二品文官，逝世後追封為一品，清同治九年（1870）建立墓碑，如今尚保存良好。墓的形制原屬完整，今尚存石象及祭台，墓之石刻仍可見當時台北附近的文人雅士及官員所寫之詩文佳句。近代其後人成立祭祀公業潘元記，負責保管維護先祖之墓園。

8. Official Residence of Chiang Kai-shek and Soong Mei-ling, Shilin
蔣中正宋美齡士林官邸

Completion Year / 1950
創建年代 / 民國三十九年

Class / National
級別 / 國定

Category / Other
類別 / 其他

Address / No.60, Fulin Rd., Shilin District, Taipei City 111
地址 / 台北市士林區福林路60號

Tel / 02-2881-2512

When ROC President Chiang Kai-shek and his wife Soong Mei-ling came to Taiwan in 1949, they lived temporarily at the Grass Mountain Guest House until a new presidential residence was completed in Shilin in 1950. Generalissimo Chiang lived in this mansion for 26 years before passing away, and thus it is the dwelling most closely associated with him and his wife. The estate on which it is located was previously an experimental botanical garden during the Japanese colonial era (1895-1945). Here,

The portrait of Madame Chiang in the Offcial Residence（士林官邸內蔣夫人的畫稿）

President Chiang hosted many leading political figures and foreign dignitaries. Kaige Chapel, built in 1949, was used for church services. Besides Chiang Kai-shek and Madame Chiang, many heads of state, high-ranking military officials and overseas guests often gathered here on Sundays. Ciyun Pavilion was built in 1963 as a memori-

The garden of the Official Residnce（士林官邸花園＊）

al to the president's mother. The main hall of the residence was a two-story cement building with dark green exterior walls. A portion of the roof was made of ceramic tiles. The ground floor features a large reception hall, while the second floor contains the bedroom and living quarters of the first couple. Although the building is of Western design, the interior maintains a traditional Chinese flavor.

The interior design of the hall of the Official Residence（士林官邸內廳堂的陳設）

The entrance way to the master room of the Official Residence（士林官邸正房入口）

　　蔣介石先生與夫人宋美齡女士於民國三十八年來台後，先居於草山行館，民國三十九年士林官邸落成時才遷入，至民國六十四年病逝前，共居住二十六年，爲其最具代表性故居，並曾在此接待各國政要。住宅四周園林環繞，景色清幽，早在日治時期即爲園藝試驗所。官邸旁之凱歌堂建於民國三十八年，當年參加禮拜者除蔣介石夫婦，受邀者大多是政府首長、高級將領或外國貴賓。慈雲亭則爲民國五十二年蔣先生爲懷念母親而建。官邸正房爲二層樓水泥構造，局部採瓦頂，外牆爲深綠色，樓下爲大會客室，二樓臥室則爲蔣先生夫婦起居空間。建築雖屬西式，但內部陳設呈現的氣氛仍保有中國傳統風格。

The interior of Kaige Chapel of the Official Residence（士林官邸凱歌堂內部空間）

9. Grass Mountain Waterworks (extends across Beitou and Shilin Districts)
草山水道系統 (此件跨區士林、北投)

Completion Year / 1928
創建年代 / 日昭和三年

Class / Municipal
級別 / 市定

Category / Other
類別 / 其他

Address / The waterworks system from Zhuzihu,
Samaoshan, Tienmu to Yuanshan
(across Beitou and Shilin Districts)

地址 / 自竹子湖經紗帽山及天母到圓山之水道設施
(跨越北投、士林兩區)

During the Mudan Village Incident of 1871, when Japanese forces first made inroads on Taiwanese soil, and the Japanese occupation of the Penghu Islands during the Sino-Japanese War of 1894, Japanese officials and soldiers suffered heavy losses from infectious diseases. Therefore, soon after Japan gained control of Taiwan in 1895, its colonial administration made great efforts to institute a public health system, a tap water system and a sewage system, in order to ensure the health of Japanese nationals living on the island.

The Taipei Waterworks System was completed in 1909, providing the predominantly Japanese districts of Taipei with tap water. Later, as the population of Taipei City rose, the volume of tap water became increasingly insufficient, and construction of the Grass Mountain Waterworks commenced in 1928. It could deliver 28,800 cubic meters of water per day, meeting the needs of 150,000 people. As the waterworks originated in the Yangming Mountains, the construction team had to overcome difficult terrain and many obstructions, making the project far more complicated than the Taipei Waterworks, headquartered in the Gongguan area.

The main facilities of the Grass Mountain Waterworks included a pumping well, aqueducts, adjustment wells, connection wells, a water main, a hydroelectric power plant and a storage reservoir. The black water main is still visible today running alongside an old stone-stepped path in Tianmu.

Above: A signpost of the Grass Mountain Waterworks erected by Taipei City Department of Cultural Affairs （台北市文化局立的「草山水道系統」招牌＊）（上圖）

Above Right: The reservoir in Yuanshan that is part of the Grass Mountain Waterworks （草山水道系統位於圓山的貯水池＊）（右頁上圖）

Below Right: The large tube on the Tube Road of Tianmu that belongs to the Grass Mountain Waterworks （草山水道系統位於天母水管路的大水管＊）（右頁下圖）

台灣總督府鑑於日本官兵於「牡丹社之役」及甲午戰爭佔領澎湖期間，因感染傳染病而死傷慘重，故於據台之初，即致力於公共衛生制度及自來水系統、排水系統之建立，以確保日人之健康。

1909年台北水道完工並供應日人分布區自來水，其後隨著台北市人口增加，自來水供水量日漸不足，於1928年動工興建草山水道。草山水道系統每日可送水量約28,800立方公尺，供給約十五萬人左右的用水量。水道工程由陽明山起始，需克服地形阻礙，且複雜的施工程度已遠超過位於公館的台北水道。

草山水道主要設施有水源取入井、水管橋、調整井、聯絡井、大水管、水力發電廠及儲水池等，現天母古道石階旁的黑色大水管，即是草山水道古蹟的一段。

10. Pan Family House, Shilin　士林潘宅

Completion Year / 1860
創建年代 / 清咸豐十年

Class / Municipal
級別 / 市定

Category / Residence
類別 / 宅第

Address / No.101, Danan Rd., Shilin District, Taipei City 111
地址 / 台北市士林區大南路101號

The ancestors of the Pan clan arrived in Taiwan during the early Qianlong era of Qing Dynasty. In late October 1859, after "Zhangzhou-Quanzhou Clash" (a battle between immigrant groups from two different areas, Zhangzhou and Quanzhou, of Fujian Province in mainland China), Pan yong-qing and Pan sheng-qing, the fourth generation of the Pan clan, marked out Shilin new street and Cixian Temple . They also participated in educational and political affairs. This well-known family is mentioned on the pillars and inscriptions of the three greatest ancient temples of Shilin.

The house, used as the ancestral shrine of the family, is not designed with extra rooms. Facing west, the house is straightly divided into a forecourt, a main entrance, a central courtyard, a hall, a mid-hall, a pavilion, a back hall, and a back gate. Because people are allowed to pass through this private house, this building, therefore, functions like a public road, which is called "Ju-guan" by neighbors.

潘氏家族於清乾隆初業攜眷渡台拓墾，其第四代潘永清、潘盛清於清咸豐九年（1859）十月末漳泉械鬥結束後規劃士林新街及慈誠宮，並興辦教育、參與政治，今日於士林三大古廟的石柱、碑記上，皆可見潘氏家族，顯其人望之盛。

Above: The brick pillars of the Pan Family House
（士林潘宅現今的磚柱＊）（上圖）

Right: The doorplate of the Pan Family House
（士林潘宅的門牌＊）（下圖）

　　潘公將此宅作爲家族公廳，未
設房間。此一座東向西之屋舍以一
直線分化成前庭、正門、中庭、大
廳、中廳、涼亭、後廳、後門，允
許有事者通行，似成一種公路的形
態，因此街民稱此屋爲「局館」。

11. The Yen Hsi-shan House　閻錫山故居

Completion Year / 1950
創建年代 / 民國三十九年

Class / Municipal　　**Category** / Residence
級別 / 市定　　　　　**類別** / 宅第

Address / No.273 and No.277, Alley 34, Lane 245,
　　　　　　Yonggong Rd., Shilin District, Taipei City 111
地址 / 台北市士林區永公路245巷34弄273號及277號

Yen Hsi-shan was born in 1883 in Wutai County, Shanxi Province. He went to Japan for formal military training in 1904. During his years in Japan, he joined Dr. Sun Yat-sen's Revolutionary Alliance, and began to advocate revolution in China. After the founding of the Chinese Republic, Yen served many important governmental positions, including military commander, military-governor, governor and government chairman of Shanxi Province, as well as ROC premier and state councilor for the ROC national government. In 1960, he died of natural causes in Taipei at the age of 77.

A view of the Yen Hsi-shan House（閻錫山故居一景＊）

A view of the Yen Hsi-shan House（閻錫山故居一景＊）

Not long after the 1945 victory of Chinese forces over Japan, the civil war between China's communist and nationalist forces broke out. In March of 1949, communist troops surrounded the walled city of Taiyuan, embroiling Yen's army in a bitter battle. Five hundred of his men ultimately sacrificed their lives defending Taiyuan from the communists.

The inscriptions on the walls of the main building of the Yen Hsi-shan House（閻錫山故居主屋牆上的碑文＊）

In March 1950, Generalissimo Chiang Kai-shek resumed the position of ROC president in Taiwan, and Yen Hsi-shan began to gradually play a less prominent role in political affairs, living a life of seclusion in this residential home in Yangmingshan. Out of a sense of homesickness, and also to protect against heat and typhoons, he had his house built into a hillside according to the yaodong style of architecture prevalent in the high plains of Shanxi Province. Here he wrote on a daily basis, and lived out the end of his days peacefully.

閻錫山，字伯川，1883年生於山西省五台縣，1904年留學日本學習軍事，留學期間加入中國同盟會，倡導革命。民國成立之後，歷任山西都督、督軍、省長、委員長、行政院長、總統府資政等要職，1960年病逝於台北，享年七十七歲。

1945年抗日戰爭勝利，不久，國共內戰爆發，1949年三月太原被共軍包圍，守軍死守太原浴血作戰，最後全軍壯烈犧牲，史稱「太原五百完人」。

1950年三月，前總統蔣介石先生在台灣復行視事，閻錫山從此逐漸淡出政壇，住在陽明山現址深居簡出，他一方面因悼念故鄉，一方面為躲避炎熱及颱風，仿山西高原窯洞建築，打造這棟石窯洞，起名「種能洞」，每日在此埋頭寫作，過著與世無爭的生活。

Above: The additional brick house to the Yen Hsi-shan House（閻錫山故居增建的磚屋＊）（上圖）

Below: The interior of the Yen Hsi-shan House（閻錫山故居室內一景＊）（下圖）

12. The White House, Tianmu (Former U.S. Military Advisors' Residence)
天母白屋（前美軍宿舍）

Completion Year / 1953
創建年代 / 民國四十二年

Class / Municipal   **Category** / Residence
級別 / 市定   **類別** / 宅第

Address / No.23, Lane 181, Sec. 7, Zhongshan N. Rd., Shilin District, Taipei City 111
地址 / 台北市士林區中山北路七段181巷23號

The White House of Tianmu originally served as a dwelling for US soldiers during the era when the American military was stationed on Taiwan. In June of 1950, with the outbreak of the Korean War, the United States came to view Taiwan as a vital part of America's line of defense in the Pacific, an "usinkable aircraft carrier." The US thus began sending its Seventh Fleet to patrol the Taiwan Strait, blocking an invasion of Taiwan by the PRC. In 1951, the US placed a detachment of military advisors on Taiwan, and the two countries signed a Mutual Defense Treaty in 1954, after which America's military presence on Taiwan increased. Subsequently, Taiwan became an indispensable ally of the United States in its efforts to halt the spread of communism during the Cold War period.

To make the life of American personnel in Taiwan pleasant and orderly, the ROC government constructed several high-quality barracks in the Shilin District, allowing American military personnel to enjoy First World standards of living in what was then a Third World country. These houses, a fusion of American and Japanese architectural styles, featured yards, external walls of white clapboard and roofs of black tile. The interiors featured fireplaces and niches built into the walls.

A close look at the White House of Tianmu（天母白屋近觀＊）

A general view of the White House of Tianmu（天母白屋外觀＊）

In 1978, the United States announced it would officially recognize the People's Republic of China, and severed formal diplomatic ties with the Republic of China. Afterwards, American military personnel left Taiwan in successive waves. Today few dwellings for American military personnel remain. The White House of Tianmu is exceptionally valuable as a showcase of this historical period, and is very worthy of preservation.

天母白屋是美軍協防台灣時期駐台人員之宿舍，1950年六月韓戰爆發，美國認為台灣是美國太平洋防線的一環，可以成為一座不能擊沉的航空母艦，開始派遣第七艦隊巡防台灣海峽，防止中共對台灣的侵略。1951年美國派遣軍事援華顧問團進駐台灣，1954年兩國簽訂「中美共同防禦條約」，駐守美軍持續增加，此後，台灣成為冷戰期間美國遏止共產主義擴張不可或缺的盟邦。

國民政府為安頓美軍在台生活，在士林地區興建許多高級眷舍，以使美軍人員雖身在第三世界，仍能享有第一世界之生活水準。這些宿舍外牆為白色雨淋板，黑色屋瓦，內設有壁爐、外露石壁龕且設有庭院，兼具美式、日式的建築風格。

1978年美國宣布將承認中共政權，並與中華民國斷絕外交關係，駐台美軍分批離開，目前留存的美軍宿舍已為數不多，天母白屋格外具有時代意義及保存價值。

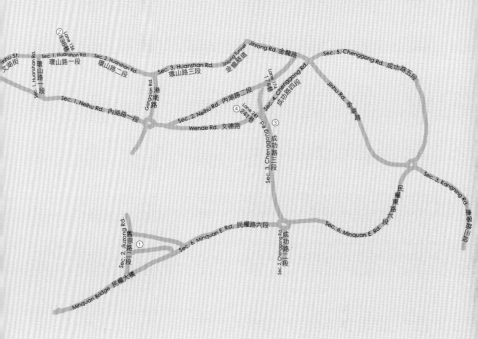

Lane 136 巷136
② 文湖街巷

Sec. 1, Huanshan Rd. 環山路一段
Huanshan St. 文湖街
Huanshan Rd. 環山路

Sec. 2, Huanshan Rd. 環山路二段

Sec. 3, Huanshan Rd. 環山路三段

Jinlong Tunnel 金龍隧道

Jinlong Rd. 金龍路

Sec. 5, Chenggong Rd. 成功路五段

Gangqian Rd. 港墘路

Sec. 1, Neihu Rd. 內湖路一段

Sec. 2, Neihu Rd. 內湖路二段

Lane 171 巷171

Sec. 4, Chenggong Rd. 成功路四段

Jinhu Rd. 金湖路

④ Lane 241 241巷

Wende Rd. 文德路

③ 成功路

Sec. 3, Chenggong Rd. 成功路三段

Sec. 3, Kangning Rd. 康寧路三段

民權東路六段

Minquan E. Rd. 民權東路六段

Sec. 2, Jiuzong Rd. 舊宗路二段

① 舊宗路二段

Sec. 6, Minquan E. Rd. 民權路六段

Sec. 2, Chenggong Rd. 成功路二段

Sec. 6, Minquan E. Rd. 民權東路六段

Minquan Bridge 民權大橋

① Tomb of Lin Xiu-jun （林秀俊墓）
② Neihu Qing Dynasty Quarry （內湖清代採石場）
③ Neihu Village Public Hall （內湖庄役場會議室）
④ Guo Family Estate （內湖郭氏古宅）

1. Tomb of Lin Xiu-jun 林秀俊墓

Completion Year / 1774
創建年代 / 清乾隆三十九年

Class / 3   **Category** / Tomb
級別 / 第三級   **類別** / 陵墓

Address / Lot No. 333, Sub-section 5, Wunde Section, Neihu District, Taipei City 114
地址 / 台北市內湖區文德段五小段333地號

The Taipei Basin was settled and developed at the beginning of the Qing dynasty by a few people from the Zhangzhou and Quanzhou areas of Fujian Province, as well as Guangdong Province. Lin Xiu-jun is considered one of the area's most important pioneers. Born in 1699, Lin Xiu-jun passed away in 1770 at the age of 72. Hailing from Zhangzhou, he immigrated to Taiwan around the age of 20. After turning 50, he took the name Lin Cheng-zu and devoted himself to developing the area from Baijiebao to Dajia'nabao – what today

A close look at the Tomb of Lin Xiu-jun
（林秀俊墓近觀）

are Banqiao, Tucheng, Yonghe, Zhonghe and Neihu. The design of his grave follows the traditional southern Fujianese style, with a hill in the center, a carved tombstone in front, and stones on either side. A short, curving wall encircles a broad court in front of the tomb. Built according to the traditional theories of Fengshui, it is one of the very few completely intact large-scale tombs from the Qing era in the Taipei Basin.

　　台北盆地是清初少數漳泉及粵人入墾所開發起來的，其中林秀俊被認為是相當重要的一位開拓先驅。林秀俊，號「成祖」，生於康熙三十八年（1699），卒於乾隆三十五年（1770），享年七十二歲。福建漳州人，弱冠離鄉來台開墾，五十歲以後自號「林成祖」，致力擺接堡及大加蚋堡一帶的墾拓與開圳，其開墾範圍包括今板橋、土城、永和、中和及內湖一帶。墓的形制採用傳統閩南式，以墓丘為中心，前置石雕墓碑，左右肩石夾立，矮垣層層彎曲伸出，呈環抱狀，前有寬廣的墓庭，格局開展，係依傳統風水理論所建，為台北盆地內少數完整保存的清代大墓。

2. Neihu Qing Dynasty Quarry　內湖清代採石場

Completion Year / 1882
創建年代 / 清光緒八年

Class / Municipal
級別 / 市定

Category / Historic Site
類別 / 遺址

Address / End of Lane 136, Huanshan Road, Neihu District, Taipei City 114
地址 / 台北市內湖區環山路136巷底

A long the outer edges of the Taipei Basin can be found high quality stone. At the end of the 19th century, the Qing government decided to construct the new city of Taipei, and chose to build its fortified wall with the andesite found in the mountains of Neihu and Dazhi. These old stones can still be seen in the culvert and walls of the former jail next to the Jinshan South Road offices of the Directorate General of Telecommunications. In addition to serving as material for the city wall, Neihu stone was also widely used as building material by the general population throughout the Japanese colonial period and following World War II. Recently, the Neihu Quarry was closed for the sake of environmental conservation. Signs of excavation are still readily visible, as is a slope specially made to slide stones down the mountain – evidence of the history of Old Taipei's construction.

A view of the Neihu Qing Dynasty Quarry（內湖清代採石場一景）

A view of Neihu Qing Dynasty Quarry（內湖清代採石場一景）

A slope trail in the site of Neihu Qing Dynasty Quarry（內湖清代採石場遺址範圍內之運石坡道景觀）

　　台北盆地周圍盛產質地優良的石材，當清末光緒年間計畫興築台北府城牆時，選擇內湖及大直一帶山區所產的安山岩作為建材。現在台北城牆的舊石料尚可在下水道及金山南路電信局旁舊監獄圍牆看到可為證。內湖山區的石料開採除了供應城牆外，一直持續到日治時期及戰後，成為民間建材來源之一。近年為保護自然生態與環境，石場已經停止開採。現場遺留許多歷年開鑿痕跡，且當年石料從山上以專闢斜坡道滑下之遺跡尚存，足為台北建城史之實證。

3. Neihu Village Public Hall （Now Neihu Community Activity Center）
內湖庄役場會議室（今內湖區民眾活動中心）

Completion Year / 1930
創建年代 / 日昭和五年

Class / Municipal
級別 / 市定

Category / Other
類別 / 其他

Address / No.342, Sec. 2, Neihu Rd., Neihu District, Taipei City 114
地址 / 台北市內湖區內湖路二段342號

Neihu Village was first established in 1920, during the Japanese colonial period. The Neihu Village Meeting Hall was built in the center of Old Neihu around 1935. The lofty roof and the entrance façade both employed architectural styles popular at that time. The meeting hall had a rectangular layout and faced north. The entrance was set in the middle of the front gable, looking out on old Neihu Village. The triangular gable contains three round windows surrounded by ornamentation. The roof ridge employs a stepped design typical of 1920s Art Deco. The horizontal entrance canopy features two semicircular pillars at its sides. Of particular interest are the light green glazed tiles with reticulated patterns on the walls. These tiles do not reflect light, and were used at that time for defense against air raids.

The entrance façade to the Neihu Village Public Hall in the old days （昔內湖庄役場會議室正面入口）

The current appearance of Neihu Village Public Hall（昔內湖庄役場會議室現貌）

The interior of the Neihu Village Public Hall（內湖庄役場會議室內景）

　　內湖在日治中期約大正九年（1920）設置內湖庄，於1935年前後建造內湖庄役場的會議室，座落內湖老市街核心地區，高大的屋頂及入口立面，採當時流行的建築式樣。內湖庄役場會議室的平面為長方形，坐南朝北，格局方整。其入口設在大山牆中央面臨內湖老街，三角形山牆上闢三個圓窗，周圍佈滿裝飾，其天際線呈階梯式造型，為典型20年代盛行的藝術裝飾主義特色。值得注意的是牆上使用不反光的網紋淺綠色釉面磚，這是當時開始運用的具有防空作用的面磚。

4. Guo Family Estate　內湖郭氏古宅

Completion Year / 1919
創建年代 / 日大正八年

Class / Municipal
級別 / 市定

Category / Residence
類別 / 宅第

Address / No.19, Lane 241, Wende Rd., Neihu District, Taipei City 114
地址 / 台北市內湖區文德路241巷19號

The home of the first Neihu Village mayor during the Japanese colonial era is located on a hill on the west side of Neihu's old district. Built circa 1919, it boasted Baroque-style embellishments, red brick, washed terrazzo, earthen sculptures and colored decorative tiles-all highly popular features of Taisho-style architecture. The house is a typical luxury home of the era. It faces south and is surrounded on three sides by woods. The ground plan of this mansion is roughly in a T formation. The predominant building materials are brick and wood. The exterior walls are made of red brick and decorated with washed terrazzo and colored tiles imported from Japan. The floor is made of wood and supported by wooden beams. Another beam was specially used to hang traditional Taiwanese censers and lanterns. The building façade's elegant curvilinear design features windows of non-uniform shape, a curved, protruding balcony and an imitation Baroque gable crest. A plaque has been added to the gable crest in recent years, naming the building Bi Feng Temple; however, it was never converted to religious use.

A view of Guo Family Estate（內湖郭氏古宅外觀一景）

A general view of Guo Family Estate which combines Eastern and Western styles（內湖郭氏古宅全景，此建物結合了漢、洋之風格）

The decorative patterns on the gable of the Guo Family Estate（內湖郭氏古宅上的裝飾紋樣）

　　內湖在日治時期首任庄長郭氏之宅邸，位於內湖市街西側山丘上。約建於日大正八年（1919），建築具有紅磚、洗石子、泥塑與彩色瓷磚裝飾等元素及當時流行巴洛克的繁飾，亦稱爲大正型建築。本宅邸即屬當時的典型豪宅。古宅坐北朝南，三面樹林環繞，形勢幽勝。古宅平面略呈 T 字形，爲磚木構造，外牆使用當時盛行的紅磚砌成，有洗石子及日本進口彩瓷裝飾。室內樓板爲木造，以木樑支撐，且有燈樑，可懸掛台灣傳統的天公爐及燈籠。正立面的窗子形式富變化，弧形凸出陽台，山頭造型仿巴洛克風格，富卷草曲線之美。山頭題額爲碧奉宮，可能因爲主人一度欲改爲寺廟，但未實現。

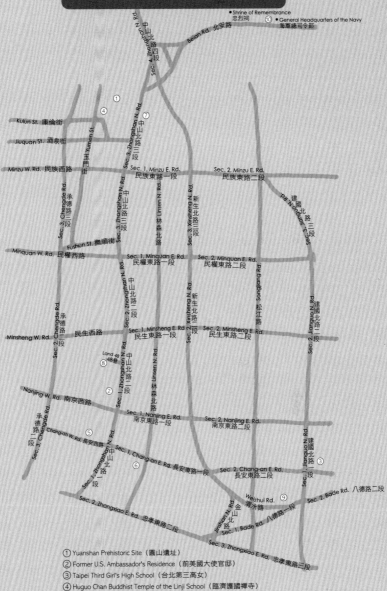

① Yuanshan Prehistoric Site （圓山遺址）
② Former U.S. Ambassador's Residence （前美國大使官邸）
③ Taipei Third Girl's High School （台北第三高女）
④ Huguo Chan Buddhist Temple of the Linji School （臨濟護國禪寺）
⑤ Old Taipei City Health Department （台北市政府衛生局舊址）
⑥ Zhongshan Presbyterian Church （中山基督長老教會）
⑦ Yuanshan Villa （圓山別莊）
⑧ Tsai Jui-yueh Dance Research Institute （蔡瑞月舞蹈研究社）
⑨ Jianguo Beer Factory （建國啤酒廠）
⑩ Qihai House （七海寓所）

Zhongshan （行政區 / 台北市中山區）

1. Yuanshan Prehistoric Site　圓山遺址

Completion Year / about 2500 years ago
創建年代 / 約2500年前

Class / 1　　　　　**Category** / Historic Site
級別 / 第一級　　　　類別 / 遺址

Address / Yumen St., Zhongshan District, Taipei City 104 (around Yuanshan)
地址 / 台北市中山區玉門街圓山一帶

The Yuanshan Prehistoric Site includes an area bounded by Zhongshan N. Rd. Section 3, Yumen St., Jiuquan St. and the Keelung River. The Taipei basin was once a lake, with the hills of Yuanshan an island rising from within it. Excavations have revealed prehistoric human activity at this location. Archaeologists have discovered an extensive mound of shells, including those of black clams, oysters, trochuses and freshwater spiral mollusks, indicating that prehistoric people discarded the shells here after eating their contents.

Further excavations have unearthed implements of clay, stone, bone and horn in an upper stratum of the site, remains of what has been named the "Yuanshan Culture." In a lower stratum, rope-patterned pottery reveals the presence of the "Dabenkeng Culture," also known as the "Rope-Pattern Terracotta Culture," one of Taiwan's earliest known Neolithic peoples.

　　遺址範圍集中於中山北路三段、玉門街、酒泉街、基隆河爲界之街廓。在台北盆地仍爲湖泊時，圓山爲湖邊小島，根據考古發掘，證實史前曾有人類在其上活動，現地發現大量貝殼，包括烏蜆殼、蠔殼、鐘螺殼及川蜷螺等，研判係史前人類食後所棄，稱爲貝塚。

　　光復後再經發掘，發現上層有陶器、石器、骨器，以及角器等出土，定名為圓山文化；在下層又發現繩紋陶，定名為繩紋陶文化，又名大坌坑文化，為台灣較早的新石器時代文化。

A general view of the fences on the Yuanshan Prehistoric Site（圓山遺址架設圍籬之今貌）（上圖）

The shells mould on the Yuanshan Prehistoric Site（圓山遺址的貝塚）（下圖）

2. Former U.S. Ambassador's Residence (Now SPOT-Taipei Film House)
前美國大使官邸 (台北之家，亦稱「光點台北」)

Completion Year / 1925
創建年代 / 民國十四年

Class / Municipal
級別 / 市定

Category / Other
類別 / 其他

Address / No.18, Sec. 2, Zhongshan N. Rd., Zhongshan District, Taipei City 104
地址 / 台北市中山區中山北路二段18號

Tel / 02-2511-7786

At the end of the nineteenth century, flourishing commerce in tea and camphor led many Western foreign countries such as the United States, the Netherlands and Britain to establish consulates and trade offices in the Dadaocheng district of Taipei. The United States built its consulate at this location during the Japanese colonial period (1895-1945). Following World War II, it served as the U.S. Ambassador's residence. Ambassadors Karl L. Rankin, Everett F. Drumright, Ian G. Kirk, Jerauld Wright, Walter P. McConaughy and Leonard Unger all made this building their home. It now stands as a historic witness to relations between Taipei and Washington, D.C.

The Former U. S. Ambassador's Residence has been transformed into SPOT-Taipei Film House.
（前美國大使官邸現在改名「光點台北」＊）

The Former U. S. Ambassador's Residence has become a place for a variety of cultural and art activities.
（前美國大使官邸現改為多元藝文活動的地點＊）

The white, two-story building was designed in a classic Western style with square floor plan, simple Grecian columns and an elegant reception hall. The original entrance faced Zhongshan North Road. The first floor functioned as administrative and reception space. The second, with a semi-covered terrace affording a pleasant view of the thoroughfare, served as living quarters for the ambassadors and their families. The residence has now been transformed into SPOT-Taipei Film House which, besides cinema screening, provides book and coffee sales, as well as services of exhibition.

清末台北因茶葉、樟腦外銷暢旺，美、荷、英等國都於大稻埕設置領事館或洋行，美國領事館日治時期遷建於此，國民政府遷台後改為美國駐華大使官邸，歷任大使藍欽、莊萊德、柯爾克、賴特、馬康衛、安克志均下榻於此，見證中美情誼。

建築方正，外觀仿洋樓設計，有簡潔的希臘柱式廊柱，梯廳精巧。原入口設於中山北路側。一樓做為行政與會客使用，二樓則為大使家人起居空間，有半露天陽台可眺望街景。今已改為多元活動的台北之家，除了放映電影，也賣書籍、咖啡或辦展覽。

3. Taipei Third Girls' High School (Now Taipei Municipal Zhongshan Girls' High School
台北第三高女（今中山女中）

Completion Year / 1937 創建年代 / 日昭和十二年	
Class / 3 級別 / 第三級	**Category** / Other 類別 / 其他
Address / No.141, Sec. 2, Chang-an E. Rd., Zhongshan District, Taipei City 104 地址 / 台北市中山區長安東路二段141號	
Tel / 02-2507-3148	

Taipei Municipal Zhongshan Girls' High School was the first girls' high school in Taiwan. Originally founded in the Shilin district of Taipei, it was later relocated to Neijiang St. in Wanhua, at which time it was renamed Taipei Third Girls' High School. Countless future leaders of society have passed through its gates.

The school is an excellent example of Taiwan's early modern design movement of the 1930s. Based on a reinforced concrete structure, its innovative design feature simply and gracefully proportioned windows and doors, an exterior blending vertical and horizontal lines, classroom corridors with lockers, and flooring of superior workmanship. It stands as a representative work of secondary educational architecture in Taiwan.

　　台灣最早的女子高級中學。初創於士林，再遷校至萬華內江街一帶，後再遷建於此，時稱「台北第三高等女學校」，作育英才無數。

　　建築反映1930年代現代設計運動興起時特徵，採用鋼筋混凝土構造，造型新穎，門窗比例簡潔優美，外觀兼具垂直與水平線條組合，教室走廊附有置物櫃，地板施工精良，咸認為具代表性的女子中學校舍。

Above and Below: The entrance to the campus of Taipei Third Girls' High School（台北第三高女校園入口景色）
（上下圖）

4. Huguo Chan Buddhist Temple of the Linji School
臨濟護國禪寺

Completion Year / 1911
創建年代 / 民國前一年

Class / Municipal
級別 / 市定

Category / Temple
類別 / 祠廟

Address / No.9, Yumen St., Zhongshan District, Taipei City 104
地址 / 台北市中山區玉門街9號

Tel / 02-2594-8308

Huguo Chan Buddhist Temple of the Linji School was founded by the Japanese Zen master Tokuan Genshu to propagate Buddhist teachings, at the invitation of the fourth Japanese governor-general of Taiwan, Kodama Gentaro. The temple took eleven years to construct, and the Linji School of Chan Buddhism (in Japanese, the Rinzai School of Zen), along with the Soto School, subsequently became a highly influential form of Buddhism in Taiwan.

Above: the Grand Sanctuary of Huguo Chan Buddhist Temple of the Linji School（臨濟護國禪寺的大雄寶殿）（上圖）

Right: The interior of the Grand Sanctuary of Huguo Chan Buddhist Temple of the Linji School（臨濟護國禪寺的大雄寶殿內殿一景）（右頁圖）

The temple, with its back against Yuanshan and Keelung River running through it, has a grand scale, awesome framework, and celestially tranquil atmosphere. The temple compound initially included a Main Gate, a Dharma Hall, a Grand Sanctuary and an Abbot's Chapel. The original Main Gate and Grand Sanctuary remain fully preserved and in good condition to the present day. The Grand Sanctuary in particular was constructed with exacting workmanship. The Huguo Chan Buddhist Temple of the Linji School is now regarded as the finest wooden temple remaining from the Japanese colonial period.

日人據台之初，總督兒玉源太郎禮聘臨濟宗日本僧人得庵玄秀禪師來台籌建，以弘法佈教，禪寺歷時十一年始落成，成爲繼曹洞宗後另一支佛教宗派，影響深遠。

禪寺背倚圓山，有基隆河蜿蜒流經，寺院開闊，格局宏整，具清幽靈毓之氣。原配置有山門、法堂、大雄寶殿及附屬方丈堂。山門、大雄寶殿悉爲創建時原作，大雄寶殿構工尤爲嚴謹，爲台灣現存日治時期木造佛寺最可觀者。

5. Old Taipei City Health Department (Now Taipei Welfare Center for the Disabled)
台北市政府衛生局舊址（今身心障礙福利會館）

Completion Year / 1930
創建年代 / 日昭和五年

Class / Municipal
級別 / 市定

Category / Other
類別 / 其他

Address / No.15, Chang-an W. Rd., Zhongshan District, Taipei City 104
地址 / 台北市中山區長安西路15號

Tel / 02-2531-7576

Originally a technical arts training center during the Japanese colonial period (1895-1945), this building was dedicated to technical training and vocational counseling to address the problem of unemployment during the Great Depression of the 1930s. It stands as a significant historical landmark of the development of social welfare services in Taipei City. Following World War II, it was transformed into a laboratory for the Taipei City Health Department.The building's European-style design is symmetrical left and right, with towers rising above both wings. A sloped roof facilitating rain drainage has now replaced the original semi-circular roof, which feature circular cavity windows and horizontal ribbon embellishments.

原為日治時期「技藝訓練所」，時適逢世界經濟不景氣，特對失業者施以技藝訓練、輔導就業，是為本市福利服務發展之歷史見證。光復後曾改為本市衛生局檢驗室。建築設計仿歐風樣式，左右對稱，兩翼設有突出高塔，屋頂上開圓洞窗，並有橫帶裝飾，整體設計饒富趣味。屋頂原是半圓筒狀，今改為斜頂，以利排水。

Above: The current appearance of the Old Taipei City Health Department（昔台北市政府衛生局今貌＊）（上圖）
Below: The entrance to the Old Taipei City Health Department（昔台北市政府衛生局入口）（下圖）

6. Zhongshan Presbyterian Church（Zhongshan Church）
中山基督長老教會（中山教會）

Completion Year / 1937
創建年代 / 日昭和十二年

Class / Municipal
級別 / 市定

Category / Church
類別 / 教堂

Address / No.62, Linsen N. Rd., Zhongshan District, Taipei City 104
地址 / 台北市中山區林森北路62號

Tel / 02-2551-8480

Originally the Taisho Street Anglican Church during the Japanese colonial period (1895-1945), this building became a Presbyterian church following World War II.

The building's distinctive architectural design is based on a cruciform floor plan running on an east-west axis. Special design features include a three-tiered bell tower, pointed arch windows and a buttress on the outer wall. Its cruciform plan features the Anglican tradition of a pulpit on the left side of the altar and a lectern, for scripture recitation by lay readers, on the right. The interior includes arched suspension roof trusses, an architectural element rarely seen in Taiwan, achieving a classically reverential atmosphere.

　　原爲日治時期基督教聖公會教堂大正町教會，提供當時鄰近街區日籍教徒禮拜之用。光復後改爲長老教會禮拜堂。
　　建築表現突出，平面呈十字形，坐西朝東，正面左側立三層鐘樓，外牆爲闊尖拱窗，設有扶壁。平面則沿襲聖公會特色，聖台左爲司會，右爲證道。室內的屋架採懸挑式拱形支撐，在台灣頗罕見，更添禮拜堂莊嚴典雅。

Above: A general view The
appearance of the
Zhongshan Presbyterian
Church（中山基督長老
教會外觀一景）（上圖）

Below: A close look at the
Zhongshan Presbyterian
Church（中山基督長老
教會外觀近景＊）（下圖）

7. Yuanshan Villa (Now Taipei Story House)
圓山別莊（今台北故事館）

Completion Year / 1914 創建年代 / 日大正三年		
Class / Municipal 級別 / 市定	**Category** / Other 類別 / 其他	
Address / No.181, Sec. 3, Zhongshan N. Rd., Zhongshan District, Taipei City 104 地址 / 台北市中山區中山北路三段181號		
Tel / 02-2587-5565		

Built as a garden retreat by wealthy businessman and Tea Merchant Association founding chairman Chen Chaojun, Yuanshan Villa first served as a reception house and family gathering place. Originally, visitors reached the villa from the district of Dadaocheng by boat via the Tamsui and Keelung rivers. Dr. Sun Yat-sen once visited here while in Taiwan. The building has had a complicated history of ownership. For a time occupied by the Japanese military police, it was also the home of former Legislative Yuan president Huang Kuo-shu following World War II.

Constructed in the English Tudor style, a rarity in Taiwan, the villa's first floor is made of brick and the second floor of wood. The posts and beams, exposed in the exterior wall, are carved in a tree-branch design. A semicircular balcony with neoclassical columns covers the entranceway, and the steeply sloping roof is graced with a central spired cupola. The intriguing rear staircase is built like a small tower, with curving eaves and arched Art Nouveau windows. Courtyards were once situated at the front and back.

Above Right: The buildings of Yuanshan Villa resemble the beautiful huts as described in fairytales. （圓山別莊的建築像童話故事中的美麗小屋＊）（右頁上圖）
Below Right: The interior of Yuanshan Villa （圓山別莊內景）（右頁下圖）

Night falls on Yuansan Villa（圓山別莊夜景）

　　大稻埕富賈、首任茶商公會理事長陳朝駿所建之花園別墅，景觀優美，招待華洋賓客及親族聚會之用，原先須搭乘小船，自大稻埕上船，沿淡水河再溯基隆河始抵達。國父孫中山先生來台時，曾到訪此地，後一度為日本憲兵隊徵用，光復後又為前立法院長黃國書寓所，歷程曲折。

　　台灣罕見都鐸式建築，一樓為紅磚結構，二樓採木構造，樑柱裸露於外牆呈樹枝狀。入口設半圓形門廊，中央凸出尖塔，屋頂急斜。背面樓梯有如一座小塔，屋頂有弧形屋簷，牆身有變體的新藝術拱形窗，饒富趣味。原先前後皆設庭院，今皆不存。

8. Tsai Jui-yueh Dance Research Institute 蔡瑞月舞蹈研究社

Completion Year / 1920
創建年代 / 日大正九年

Class / Municipal
級別 / 市定

Category / Other
類別 / 其他

Address / No.8 and No.10, Lane 48, Sec. 2, Zhongshan N. Rd., Zhongshan District, Taipei City 104,
地址 / 台北市中山區中山北路二段48巷8、10號

The Tsai Jui-yueh Dance Research Institute building was originally a dormitory for government employees during the era of Japanese colonial period. The houses in this predominantly Japanese neighborhood were arranged in orderly rows and of uniform size. Following World War II, many officials of the Republic of China, included such renowned individuals as Huang Chi-ruey and Huang Chao-ching, took abode in this district.

A view of the garden in the Tsai Jui-yueh Dance Research Institute
(蔡瑞月舞蹈研究社花園環境)

After studying dance in Japan, Ms. Tsai Jui-Yueh embarked on a career in dance instruction, founding the Chung-hua Dance Research Institute in 1953. Internationally recognized as a choreographer and performer, she composed over two hundred works and was versatile in ballet, modern dance and traditional folk dance. She is highly regarded as an educator and a pioneer promoter of modern dance in Taiwan. Damaged by fire in October 1999, the building has now been restored to its original appearance.

Above: A view of the Tsai Jui-yueh Dance Research Institute
（蔡瑞月舞蹈研究社屋舍一景）（上圖）

Below: A dance course in the Tsai Jui-yueh Dance Research Institute（蔡瑞月舞蹈研究社練舞的情形）（下圖）

建物原為日治時期公務員宿舍，鄰近街廓為當時本市日人集中的住宅區，建築排列整齊且規模相當。光復後延續作為政府官員宿舍，包括聞人黃啓瑞、黃朝琴等都曾住在此區。

舞蹈家蔡瑞月女士二次大戰期間赴日習舞，學成後返台積極從事舞蹈教學。民國四十二年起於此設立「中華舞蹈研究社」進行舞蹈教學、創作表演、國際交流，編過近兩百件舞作，表現型態涵蓋芭蕾、現代、民族舞蹈，在國內舞蹈教育與現代舞推廣上貢獻卓越，培育許多傑出人才。舞蹈社於民國八十八年十月間遭人縱火破壞，今依原樣重行修復。

9. Jianguo Beer Factory 建國啤酒廠

Completion Year / 1920
創建年代 / 日大正九年

Class / Municipal
級別 / 市定

Category / Other
類別 / 其他

Address / No85, Sec. 2, Bade Rd., Zhongshan District, Taipei City 104
地址 / 台北市中山區八德路二段85號

Originally established under the Japanese colonial government, the Jianguo Beer Factory's predecessor, the Takasago Beer Company, was the first brewery in Taiwan and enjoyed prestige on a par with the Sapporo Brewery of Hokkaido, Japan. Expanded in the 1960s, the Jianguo Beer Factory achieved an output of over 144 million bottles, its quality lager winning international awards including the Monde Selection award of Belgium.

The original complex featured a mixture of structures made of redbrick, stone and steel-reinforced concrete. Later additions were primarily brick wall and steel truss structures, reflecting the evolution of construction technology. Though now decommissioned, much of the facility's equipment remains on-site, as historical evidence of the development of Taiwan's brewing industry.

The copper facilities in the Jianguo Beer Factory （建國啤酒廠銅製設備）

前身爲高砂麥酒株式會社，爲台灣第一座啤酒製造工廠，與日本北海道札幌啤酒廠齊名。民國五○年代開始擴建，最高產量曾達到一千二百多萬打，並多次奪得國際啤酒品評會大獎，釀造品質優異。

　　創建時廠房屬紅磚、石材與鋼骨混合之構造，爾後增建者，則以磚牆及鋼鐵桁架結構爲主，反映時代技術演替。廠區生產機具設備仍續予保留，見證台北釀酒產業發展。

Above: A distant view of the Jianguo Beer Factory（建國啤酒廠俯瞰）（上圖）

Below: The red building of the Jianguo Beer Factory served as the brewing room during the Japanese colonial period.（建國啤酒廠的紅樓在日治時代爲糖化室）（下圖）

10. Qihai House（Former Residence of Late President Chiang Ching-kuo）
七海寓所（蔣經國故居）

Completion Year / 1950s-1960s
創建年代 / 民國三十九至四十九年間

Class / Municipal   **Category** / Residence
級別 / 市定   **類別** / 宅第

Address / Dachi Barracks, the Headquarters of Chinese Navy, Zhongshan District, Taipei City 104
地址 / 台北市中山區海軍總司令大直營區

Situated at the foot of the hill Yuanshan, this western-style, steel RC building, according to historical records, was built in the 1950s or 1960s based on a modern architecture layout with a circular driveway lined with gardens in its front yard. This not-very-old residence commonly known as "Qihai House," though somewhat aging, is well-preserved with a relatively high quality in term of its style, environment and atmosphere.

The small living room near the entrance of Qihai House（七海寓所一樓進門小客廳一景＊）

The 2-story mansion had been the official residence of late President Chiang Ching-kuo since he began using in 1969. The first floor provided meeting quarters for receiving foreign VIPs and the family members while the second floor comprised his office and the living rooms for him and Ms. Chiang Fang-liang. The simple and plain interior reflects how the Chiang couple lived their everyday life and how frugal they used to be.

本建物依文獻記載，為1950年至1960年新式鋼筋混凝土建築，採西式現代建築佈局依山而建，前有圓形迴車花圃，年代雖不算久，但現況保存良好，其格局、環境皆有一定品質。

七海寓所之前為蔣經國先生故居，其自1969年遷居至此寓所，一樓用來會見外賓、家族聚會使用，二樓則是辦公與夫人蔣方良女士日常起居的空間，內部生活空間，呈現出當時蔣先生家居生活與精神的面貌。

The restaurant in the first floor of Qihai House （七海寓所一樓餐廳一景。＊）

Datong

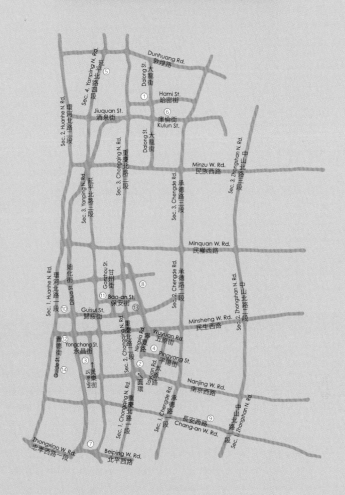

① Dalongdong Baoan Temple（大龍峒保安宮）

② Dadaocheng Traffic Circle Air Defense Reservoir（大稻埕圓環防空蓄水池）

③ Xia Hai Cheng Huang Temple of City God（大稻埕霞海城隍廟）

④ Chen Dexing Ancestral Shrine（陳德星堂）

⑤ Chen Yueji Ancestral Mansion（陳悅記祖宅）

⑥ Taipei Confucius Temple（台北孔廟）

⑦ The Railway Division of Taiwan Governor General's Bureau of Transportation（台灣總督府交通局鐵道部）

⑧ Old Police Headquarter of Northern Precinc（原台北市警察署）

⑨ Old Taipei City Hall（台北市政府舊廈）

⑩ Dadaocheng Gu's Family Mansion（大稻埕辜宅）

⑪ Dadaocheng Presbyterian Church（台灣基督長老教會）

⑫ Chen Tian-Lai Residence（陳天來故居）

⑬ Uen Meng Building on Guisui Street（歸綏街文萌樓）

⑭ Dadaocheng Qianqiu Street Stores（大稻埕千秋街店屋）

Datong （行政區 / 台北市大同區）

1. Dalongdong Baoan Temple　大龍峒保安宮

Completion Year / 1805
創建年代 / 清嘉慶十年

Class / 2　　　　**Category** / Temple
級別 / 第二級　　　類別 / 祠廟

Address / No.61, Hami St., Datong District, Taipei City 103
地址 / 台北市大同區哈密街61號

Tel / 02-2595-1676

During the Qian Long period of the Qing Dynasty, people of Tong-an from Quan Zhou of Fu Jian Province first immigrated down the Tam Shui River settling in the Dalongdong area of Taipei. Later in the mid-Qing years as the economy grew greatly, many became rich enough to build temples to give thanks to their gods. The Tongan settlers chiefly worshiped King Bao Sheng Da Di (a title conferred by the then Emperor) named Wu Ben, generally known as "Dao gong" or "Wu Zhen Ren (an enlightened Daoist)," who is respected by local people as God of Medicine. Baoan Temple, a spiritual branch of the host temple at Bai Jiao Village, Tongan County of Quan Zhou, began construction in the 10th year of the Jia Qing period of the Qing Dynasty (1805); it was completed in the 10the year of the Dao Guang period (1830).

The grand temple complex comprises the entrance or front hall, main hall and rear hall with its layout shaped like the Chinese character "回." The wide façade of the front hall contains 5 rooms plus the East and West Wings with its double-eave mountain-shape roofs. The independent main hall is in the highest class of its style. In the 6th year of Emperor O-sho period of the Japanese rule (1917), large-scale renovations were made by two teams of carpenters respectively led by Masters Chen Ying-bin and Guo Ta hired to compete with each other to show their skilled features with the main hall divided into two halves from the central line.

The wall paintings of the main hall are the works in 1973 by Master Pan Li-shui, an accomplished painter from Tainan. Every year, on the 15th day of the 3rd moon on the lunar calendar, to celebrate the birthday of King Bao Sheng Da Di, noisy processions and festivals are held in his honor that has become the most spectacular folk event in Taipei. In recent years the Baoan Temple has been doing its renovations with chosen materials in so strict and meticulous a fashion that it now sets an example for others to learn from in terms of preserving a traditional temple.

Above: The interior of the front hall of Baoan Temple（保安宮前殿大廳＊）（上圖）

Below: The front hall of Baoan Temple（保安宮前殿一景＊）（下圖）

清乾隆年間福建泉州府同安人，溯淡水河到大龍峒地區開墾，到清代中葉開發穩定，社會富足有足夠經濟能力來興建大廟。同安人信奉保生大帝吳本，俗稱大道公或吳眞人，民間尊爲醫神。本廟自泉州同安縣白礁鄉分靈來台，清嘉慶十年（1805）保安宮開始建廟，清道光十年（1830）建成。

廟宇佈局宏偉，包含前、後殿及正殿，平面呈回字型，前殿面寬五開間，屋頂使用歇山重簷型式，莊嚴華麗。正殿獨立，爲廟宇等級之最高型式。大正六年（1917）大修時，由陳應彬與郭塔兩位名師對場興修，由正殿中線對分，各自發揮木作特色。

正殿壁畫爲台南名師潘麗水於民國六十二年（1973）所繪。每年農曆三月十五日爲保生大帝神誕，迎神賽會爲台北的民俗盛事。近年來保安的修繕工程施工嚴謹，材料講究，爲傳統廟宇修繕之典範。

2. Dadaocheng Traffic Circle Air Defense Reservoir
(Taipei Traffic Circle Resovoir)
大稻埕圓環防空蓄水池 (圓環蓄水池)

Completion Year / 1943
創建年代 / 日昭和十八年

Class / Municipal   **Category** / Other
級別 / 市定   **類別** / 其他

Address / Jiancheng Circle, Datong District, Taipei City 103
地址 / 台北市大同區建成圓環內

Above : The Current appearance of the Dadaocheng Traffic Circle Air Defense Reservoir (大稻埕圓環防空蓄水池現況外觀＊) (上圖)

Below : The red-bricked Dadaocheng Traffic Circle Air Defense Reservoir (大稻埕圓環防空紅磚蓄水池) (下圖)

Situated at the intersection of Chongqing North Road and Nanjing West Road overlapping the traffic circle, this historical site is, to this day, the largest sized cistern or water storage project conceived to counter air raid ever exhumed in Taiwan. From the 1920s on, peddlers and hawkers began gathering in the neighborhood, contributing to the commerical boom of the area of profound historical  significance. The prosperity lasted until 1943, when the U. S. Air Force began bombarding Taiwan, the authorities decided to prohibit commercial activities in the area. Giant cistern were dug, instead, for the purpose of providing water for extinguishing possible fires caused by air raids. After World War II, the circle market area gradually restored its earlier vigor, and evolved into a hustle and bustle night market.

　　此古蹟爲目前台北市僅有出土之最大的防空蓄水池，位於重慶北路與南京西路交口之圓環位置，極具歷史價值，在1920年代，小販開始聚集於此，商業興盛。到了1943年，美軍轟炸台灣，圓環攤販的商業行爲也開始被政府禁止，並在圓環中央開挖防空蓄水池，以供空襲發生火災時汲水滅火。二次大戰後，圓環才逐漸恢復昔時盛景，並形成繁華夜市。

3. Xia Hai Cheng Huang Temple of City God
大稻埕霞海城隍廟

Completion Year / 1859
創建年代 / 清咸豐九年

Class / 3
級別 / 第三級

Category / Temple
類別 / 祠廟

Address / No.61, Sec. 1, Dihua St., Datong District, Taipei City 103
地址 / 台北市大同區迪化街一段61號

Tel / 02-2558-0346

Cheng Huang or City God Xia Hai, originally worshiped as a god of garrison or guard or the local magistrate of the underworld, people of Wu Xiang Zhuang of Xia Dian Village in Tong An County, Quan Zhou in Fu Jian Province. In the Dao Guang years of the Qing Dynasty, Chen Jin-rong, a follower of the guard god, came to Taiwan to establish a branch temple at the Ba Jia Zhuang to the east of the then downtown Manka. In the 3rd year of Xian Fong period (1953), the temple was destroyed because of armed clashes

The splendidly lighted Xia Hai Cheng Huang Temple in the evening（大稻埕霞海城隍廟夜間燈火輝煌＊）

at the Ding Xia suburb between immigrants from different areas of mainland China. The devotees temporarily placed the salvaged City God at the "Jin Tong Li Cake Shop," owned by Chen Hao-ran, a native of Da Dao Cheng. Three years later, at the urging of the followers, the temple was rebuilt at the extant site on the land donated by a Mr. Su in the 9th year of the Xian Fong period of Qing Dynasty (1959) whereas

The interior of Xia Hai Cheng Huang Temple（大稻埕霞海城隍廟內部一景＊）

City God Xia Hai was worshiped as the head god, accompanied by idols and images of 38 heroes who had sacrificed themselves for escorting the saved city god from Manka to Dadaocheng.

This temple, comprised a main hall and a worship pavilion, is small in scale. However, it has had attracted a great number of worshippers and pilgrims, especially on the 13th day of 5th lunar month, when a ceremony is held to celebrate the city god's birthday. This ceremony, which gains increasing attention with time, gives rise to the saying "On 5/13, People, People, Everywhere." In recent years, a series of renovations have been conceived to restore the temple to its original look. On both sides of the main hall are well-preserved lifelike Koji pottery green dragon and white tiger, both being the works of master ceramicist Chen Tien-qi. Their impeccability is rarely seen in the pottery works in other temples around the neighborhood of Taipei.

霞海城隍，原係福建泉州同安下店鄉五鄉莊居民鎮守之神，清道光年間由信徒陳金絨等奉靈來台，初建廟於艋舺市區東邊的八甲莊，咸豐三年（1853）因頂下郊拼，毀於兵災，信徒從火焰中救出神像，暫時安置於大稻埕陳浩然「金同立餅舖」中。三年後信眾倡議擇地建廟，地主蘇氏協台捐獻廟地，咸豐

九年（1859）建廟於現址。奉祀霞海城隍主神，並配祀三十八位當年自艋舺護送神像至大稻埕途中受襲死難的義勇公。

　　本廟只有正殿與拜亭，格局雖小但香火鼎盛，每年農曆五月十三日祭典盛況空前，有「五月十三人看人」之美譽。近年經過整修已經恢復原貌。正殿內左右牆尚保存名匠陳天乞的交趾陶，左邊為青龍，右邊為白虎，姿態栩栩如生，為目前台北附近古廟所存少數完整無瑕之傑作。

Above 4 pictures: The inscriptions of the words "Taipei Xia Hai Cheng Huang Lao Ye" on the door tablet of Xia Hai Cheng Huang Temple （霞海城隍廟門匾上的「台北霞海城隍老爺」字樣）（上四圖）

Below: The pottery carving in Xia Hai Cheng Huang Temple （霞海城隍廟內陶雕＊）（下圖）

4. Chen Dexing Ancestral Shrine 陳德星堂

Completion Year / 1892
創建年代 / 清光緒年間

Class / 3　　　　　**Category** / Temple
級別 / 第三級　　　**類別** / 祠廟

Address / No.27, Ningxia Rd., Datong District, Taipei City 103
地址 / 台北市大同區寧夏路27號

Chen Dexing Ancestral Shrine, Taipei's No. 1 ancestral shrine in terms of clan size, was originally located within the ancient walled city of Taipei during the Guang Xu years of the Qing Dynasty. Early in the Japanese rule, in order to build the Office of Taiwan Governor General, the authorities took over the original site in exchange for a land reserved for armed force which was located in the Da Dao Cheng area. There at the current location, the Chens rebuilt their clan shrine in the 1st year of O-sho period (1912) which was inaugurated two years later.

Left: The tin vase and light holder preserved in Chen Dexing Ancestral Shrine are rarely seen throughout Taiwan.
（陳德星堂內保存的錫製花瓶與燈台全台罕見）（左圖）

Right: A general view of Chen Dexing Ancestral Shrine
（陳德星堂外觀＊）（右頁圖）

The Shrine was designed and constructed by a famous master carpenter named Chen Ying-bin. This beautiful traditional architecture is decorated with exquisitely elaborate carvings, especially for its double-eave, mountain-shape roofs, mortis and tenon wood structure, and dou gong, or bucket arch - a column and beam bracketing system. The flowing style of both its eaves and roof ridge are highly artistic and aesthetic. The two stone columns each carved with a double dragon in front of the entrance hall are believed to be the earliest version of a double-dragon column seen in Taiwan's contemporary architecture; they profoundly affected the later generation's temple building. In the main hall, the altar holding the tablets of ancestors are immense in size and magnificently rich in delicate wood carving, with featured by the meticulously sculpted railings. In front of the tablet altar, the sacrificial utensils or vases of tin ware and fairy-shaped candle stands remain intact coming in a requisite form that is rarely seen elsewhere on Taiwan.

陳德星堂爲台北地區陳氏大宗祠，清光緒年間原在台北府城內。日治初年日本政府徵用祠堂原址作爲建造總督府用地，並以大稻埕的陸軍用地交換。陳氏族人後於大正元年（1912）興工重建，兩年後於現址落成啓用。

此堂爲台灣著名匠師陳應彬設計建造，建築造型優美，雕琢細膩。尤其是前殿的重簷歇山式屋頂、木結構及斗拱精美，屋簷及屋脊曲線流暢，具有很高的藝術價值。前殿石雕雙龍柱，被認爲是近代台灣較早出現一柱雙龍之例，對後來的寺廟興建有深遠的影響。正殿內神龕尺寸巨大，木雕豐富，以精雕的鉤欄爲其特點。龕前的錫製祭具與仙人燭台保存完整，造型精湛，爲台灣罕見之例。

5. Chen Yueji Ancestral Mansion（Old Master's Mansion）
陳悅記祖宅（老師府）

Completion Year / 1807
創建年代 / 清嘉慶十二年

Class / 3
級別 / 第三級

Category / Temple
類別 / 祠廟

Address / No.231, Sec. 4, Yanping N. Rd., Datong District, Taipei City 103
地址 / 台北市大同區延平北路四段231號

Chen Yueji Ancestral Mansion, the old residence of Taipei's well-known Confucian Scholar Chen Wei-ying nicknamed "Yueji," is a symbol of the heyday of education and civilization of the Dalongdong area in the Qing Dynasty. In the 9th year of Xian Feng period of the Qing Dynasty (1859), Chen Wei-ying, having successfully passed the province-level imperial examination to become a Ju Ren, started his lifelong devotion to the advancement of culture and education in the Dalongdong area, where, as a result of his efforts, more talents and scholars gathered than elsewhere, so went a fame for "Xiu Cai and Ju Ren, who passed the imperial exams, are everywhere down the Street!" He was the master teacher of Min county, and Head of Manka Xue Hai Academy and Yilan Yang Shan Academy, and respected by locals as "Old Master," thus his residence also known as "Old Master's Mansion."

The renovated images of Door Gods of the residence（整修後的老師府門神＊）

Above: A view of the Chen Yueji Ancetsral Mansion（老師府一景）（上圖）
Below 2 pictures: The doorplate of the Chen Yueji Ancestral Mansion（老師府門牌＊）（下兩圖）

The original mansion was built in the 12th year of Jia Qing period of the Qing Dynasty (1807) and renovated early in the Xian Fong period. The whole structure with a single ridge and a swallow tail-shaped roof consists of 3 main houses in a row with 2 wings. The family shrine, also known as Hall of the Ancestors, is located on the left side of the entrance; on the right side is Hall for the House for receiving guests. The 3rd row house and guarding wings on either side are for residential use. In front of the mansion, there used to be a pair of tone flag poles and a wooden poles symbolizing the honor of being a Ju Ren; now only the stone pole stands remain – rather valuable relics as the only extant pair to be seen on Taiwan now.

A view of the Chen Yueji Ancetsral Mansion（老師府一景）

The stone flag erected in front of the Chen Yueji Ancestral Mansion（老師府前埕所立的石雕旗杆）

陳悅記祖宅爲台北名儒陳維英之家宅，它是大龍峒地區清代文風鼎盛的象徵。陳維英於清咸豐九年（1859）考中舉人，一生致力於振興文教，使大龍峒名士輩出，有「五步一秀，十步一舉」的美譽。曾任閩縣教喻、艋舺學海書院和宜蘭仰山書院院長，地方人士尊爲「老師」，稱其宅爲「老師府」。

原建築創建於清嘉慶十二年（1807），咸豐初年重修，由單脊式燕尾屋頂之三落與四落大厝兩棟並列而成，入口左側爲家祠，俗稱公媽廳，右側爲接待賓客的公館廳，第三進及兩側護龍則爲住宅。前埕原立有象徵科舉功名榮譽之石旗杆及木旗杆各一對，現木旗杆僅剩夾杆石礎，石旗杆仍存，全台灣僅此一對，相當珍貴。

6. Taipei Confucius Temple   台北孔廟

Completion Year / 1925 **創建年代** / 日大正十四年		
Class / 3 **級別** / 第三級	**Category** / Temple **類別** / 祠廟	
Address / No.275, Dalong St., Datong District, Taipei City 103 **地址** / 台北市大同區大龍街275號		
Tel / 02-2592-3934		

Confucius was born in the last years of the Spring and Autumn Period. A man of great learning who believed in and promoted his belief of "Education for All without Distinction, he is revered as the greatest sage and teacher by the later generations. To commemorate this great sage teacher, the Confucius Temples were built in important cities where, every year on September 28, Confucius' Birthday, the Confucius Ceremony is held within the temple.

The Taipei Confucius Temple was originated in the 5th year of the Guang Xu period of the Qing Dynasty (1879) erecting side by side with the Martial Temple (in honor of God of War Guan Yu). In the early years of the Japanese reign, the major portion of the temple and its chambers were repeatedly ravaged by war. In the 14th year of Emperor O-sho (1925), gentry and scholar-officials in Taipei proposed rebuilding the Confucius Temple; they invited the famous carpenter Wang Yi-shun from Quan Zhou to design and construct it. In the 5th year of Emperor Showa (1930), the Yi Gate, Da Cheng Hall, Chong Sheng Shrine and East and West Wings were completed and the first Confucius Ceremony was held. The remaining structures of the temple were not completed until the 14th year of Emperor Showa (1939) when sufficient donations were collected.

Dacheng Hall of the Taipei Confucius Temple （台北市孔廟大成殿＊）

The architecture of Taipei Confucius Temple is modelled on the Chinese ancient norm of architecture which has a fully developed set of methods and techniques. The octagonal ceiling caissons in the Dacheng Hall, for example, have won long and wide admiration from visitors, both home and abroad. Its Quan Zhou style of mortise-tenon wood connecting crafts characterizes that of contemporary Taiwanese architecture.

　　孔子生於春秋末年，學識淵博，有教無類，後人尊為至聖先師。孔廟為紀念孔子的地方，每年九月二十八日孔子誕辰於孔廟內舉行祭孔大典。

　　台北原有孔廟，建於清光緒五年（1879），當時位於城內與武廟並列，日治初期遭兵災，殿廡毀損嚴重。大正十四年（1925）台北士紳倡議重建孔廟，聘請泉州名匠王益順來台設計建造，於昭和五年（1930）建儀門、大成殿、崇聖祠及兩廡，並舉行祭典，後因捐款頓挫直到昭和十四年（1939）才完成其餘建築。

　　台北孔子廟遵照中國古建築手法興建，規制完備，建築技巧精良，例如大成殿內的八角藻井一向為中外人士所讚美，是近代台灣最典型的泉州木結構風格之建築。

Above 2 pictures: The bell and drum in the Taipei Confucius Temple（台北市孔廟內的鐘和鼓＊）（左上圖和右上圖）

Below Left: The Confucius Memorial Ceremony hosted in the Taipei Confucius Temple（台北市孔廟祭孔儀式一景）（左下圖）

Below Right: The entrance to the Taipei Confucius Temple（台北市孔廟入口＊）（右下圖）

7. The Railway Division of Taiwan Governor General's Bureau of Transportation (Former Location of Taiwan Railway Administration)
台灣總督府交通局鐵道部 (台鐵舊舍)

Completion Year / 1919
創建年代 / 大正八年

Class / 3　　　　**Category /** Other
級別 / 第三級　　**類別 /** 其他

Address / No.2, Sec. 1, Yanping N. Rd., Datong District, Taipei City 103
地址 / 台北市大同區延平北路一段2號

Situated outside of the northern gate, the Railway Division of Taiwan Governor General's Bureau of Transportation, formerly the Bureau of Machinery responsible for machinery manufacture and train repairs during Liu Ming-chuan's administration late in the Qing Dynasty, was the locomotive of Taiwan's industrial modernization. In the early years of the Japanese rule, the site was allocated for the use of the Railway Division; in the 8th year of Emperor O-sho (1919), the present Railway Division Building was renamed Taiwan Railway Administration after the island restored sovereignty from Japanese Occupation.

The Building was designed by Moniyama Matsu, an architect with the Civil Engineering Bureau of the Office of Governor General, whose important works included Taipei Prefecture Hall (now the Control Yuan building), Taichung Prefecture Hall and Taiwan Prefecture Hall. The feature of his comprehensive architectural style lies in the combined use of brick and wood as commonly seen in the 19th century Victorian structure: the house on the ground or 1st floor was made of brick to provide a solid foundation while that on the second floor was of lighter-weight wooden structure. Noteworthy is that all wooden beams and pillars were made of the cypress wood produced in Mt. Ali. Other highlights include plastered ceiling and wall exquisitely sculpted and recycled railways ingeniously used as construction materials for local interior deco.

A general view of the Railway Division of Taiwan Governor General's Bureau of Transportation（台灣總督府交通局鐵道部外貌）

The interior of the Railway Division of Taiwan Governor General's Bureau of Transportation（台灣總督府交通局鐵道部內景）

　　位於北門外的台灣總督府交通局鐵道部，在清末劉銘傳主政時期爲機器局，負責製造機械及修理火車，是台灣近代工業的起點。日治初期改爲鐵道部用地，於大正八年（1919）建成鐵道部大樓，台灣光復後改爲台灣省鐵路局。

　　建築的設計者爲台灣總督府土木局營繕課的建築技師森山松之助，其重要作品有台北州廳（今監察院）、台中州廳及台南州廳等。整體建築風格較爲特殊，採用十九世紀維多利亞時期之磚木混合結構，一樓用穩重之紅磚疊砌，二樓爲較輕盈的木造結構。值得一提的是整體木造柱樑及屋架結構大部分使用阿里山所產之檜木。其他如做工精細的灰泥雕塑，以及利用廢鋼軌轉作爲局部室內建材，充分展現創意巧思。

8. Old Police Headquarter of Northern Precinct (Now Datong District Police Bureau)
原台北北警察署（今大同分局）

Completion Year / 1933
創建年代 / 日昭和八年

Class / Municipal   **Category** / Government Office
級別 / 市定   類別 / 衙署

Address / No.89, Ningxia Rd., Datong District, Taipei City 103
地址 / 台北市大同區寧夏路89號

Tel / 02-2557-7262

Under the Japanese colonial rule, Taipei Police Administration was divided into the southern and northern precincts. The Police Headquarters of Northern Precinct was set up in Dadaocheng to maintain law and order, because it had the largest concentration of native Taiwanese. It is also the economic and commercial center of northern Taiwan at that time.

In the last years of the Japanese occupation, Dadaocheng area was the cradle of Taiwan's democratic, political and social movements, for which many Taiwanese elite and talents advocating their beliefs and ideals against the Office of the Governor General, were detained in the Police Headquarters of Northern Precinct. The famous Medical Doctor Chiang Wei-shui had been in and out the headquarters four times, authoring some articles in the then *Taiwan Min Bao* or *Taiwanese Newspaper*, telling stories about the Taiwanese kept in prison there.

This structure, designed by the Division of Governmental Office Construction of the Office of Taiwan Governor General, looks unadorned and practical. On the corner of the building facing the street, it has an arc wall with its double-paneled side window which is semi-circular shaped. It is a rare remainder of similar police stations which were of relatively large scale built under the Japanese rule. The original internal facilities, such as detention units and water prison, are retained to show the specific space or function needs.

　日治時期的台北警察署分爲南署與北署，北署位於大稻埕，以該區多爲台灣人聚居並爲北台灣經濟重心，爲控制治安而設置。

　大稻埕地區爲日治末期台灣民主政治社會運動的發源地，許多台籍菁英因鼓吹其理念，不見容於日總督府而被捕，監禁於北警署。名醫蔣渭水即曾出入該警署達四次，於獄中著有拘禁台灣人之觀察文章，發表於當時的台灣民報。

　此建築物由總督府官房營繕課設計，外觀平實，臨街轉角爲弧面牆，側邊牆重覆之半圓拱窗，是目前台北市僅存日治時期較具規模的警察局。內部保留原設計之拘留所及水牢，呈現警察局特殊空間機能要求。

A view of Datong District Police Bureau, the former Police Headquarter of Northern Precinct （原台北北警察署即今大同分局，圖爲現貌。＊）

9. Old Taipei City Hall (Now Museum of Contemporary Art Taipei)
台北市政府舊廈（原建成小學校，今台北當代藝術館）

Completion Year / 1921
創建年代 / 日大正十年

Class / Municipal
級別 / 市定

Category / Other
類別 / 其他

Address / No.39, Chang-an W. Rd., Zhongshan District, Taipei City 104
地址 / 台北市大同區長安西路39號

Tel / 02-2552-3720

The Old Taipei City Hall was originally the site for the Jian Cheng General Elementary School under the Japanese rule, where most of the students were from the Japanese families. The structure was built following the then typical elementary school layout modeled on the shape of a Mandarin Chinese phonetic symboll "ㄩ;" the inside of it is a sport field surrounded on three sides by arched corridors. In the early years of Taiwan's restoration, it was assigned to be the office building for the Taipei City Hall and had since become an important landmark in the citizens' mind for some time.

A corridor in the Old Taipei City Hall（台北市政府舊廈內景長廊）

With the fast growth of municipal Taipei whose seat was moved to the newly built, larger premise in the Xinyi District, the front building of the old Taipei City Hall, now the location for Museum of Contemporary Art Taipei, is connected to the rear building as an art exhibition and art education center collaborated with the adjourning Jian Cheng Junior High School – a rare example of the joint-venture space utilization. The layout of this brick structure is symmetrically patterned with a central entrance leading to the lobby and the second floor conference hall and another two entrances – one each on the left and right sides. The interior of the house is spacious with relatively high ceiling, on the central top of which, a bell tower is installed to stand out as an eye-catching focus.

　　台北市政府舊廈原爲日治時期「建成尋常小學校」，當年學童多爲日人子弟，整體平面建築爲ㄩ字形，內側設拱廊圍繞操場，爲當時常見的小學配置方式。光復初期充爲台北市政府辦公廳舍後，長期成爲市民心中重要的地標。

　　隨著台北市的發展，市政府遷往信義區的新市政中心，原有前棟建築改爲當代藝術館，與後棟建成國中結合成難得的藝術展覽與教育共構空間。本建築爲紅磚造左右對稱配置，中央及左右側各設入口，中央入口大廳的二樓爲大集會廳，室內空間跨度大且天花板較高，其上並設計一座突出的鐘樓成爲醒目的視覺焦點。

Above: A bird's eye view of the Old Taipei City Hall（台北市政府舊廈鳥瞰）（上圖）

Below: A general view of the Old Taipei City Hall（台北市政府舊廈外觀＊）（下圖）

10. Dadaocheng Gu's Family Mansion (Now Rong Shing Kindergarten)
大稻埕辜宅 （今榮星幼稚園）

Completion Year / around 1920
創建年代 / 日大正九年前後

Class / Municipal
級別 / 市定

Category / Residence
類別 / 宅第

Address / No.9, Lane 303, Guisui St., Datong District, Taipei City 103
地址 / 台北市大同區歸綏街303巷9號

Tel / 02-2553-6699

In the last years of the Qing Dynasty, on both sides of the banks of the Dadaocheng section of Tamsui River were lined with foreign trading firms and embassies, thus making this area the busiest center of booming trade and business on Taiwan. There a great number of wealthy merchants chose to live in their huge, western-style houses.

At the early stage of the Japanese colonial rule, a wealthy merchant named Gu Xian-rong, granted the right of monopoly in selling the government-produced salt, first built a salt business office and, behind it a 3-story mansion on the water front of the Tam Shui River. After the restoration of Taiwan to the Republic of China, the property had been used by the famous Rong Xing (Rong Shing or Glorious Star) Chorus until it was transferred to its present user - Rong Xing Kindergarten in the 53rd year of the ROC (1963).

An imitation of European-style architecture in the peak of the Renaissance period, the elevation drawing has an excellent ration of division with its light-colored tiled walls, decorated with exquisitely elegant relief out of the cobbled hard surface – displaying an impressive, extravagant lifestyle of the rich businessmen at that time. Inside the large house, both the ceilings and stair railings are made of cypress wood,

complete with a refined marble fireplace. All are well-preserved; the heyday of Dadaocheng is gone now, but many reminders of its glory days remain.

大稻埕沿淡水河岸碼頭，清末洋行領事館林立，因貿易成為全台最繁榮的地區之一，吸引不少富商購建洋樓豪宅於此地。

日治初期富商辜顯榮取得台灣官鹽專賣權後，於淡水河畔建築鹽館辦公室及後棟的三層樓住宅。台灣光復後曾為著名的榮星合唱團所使用，民國五十二年（1963）以後為幼稚園使用。

此建築仿西洋文藝復興式風格，立面有極佳的分割比例，外牆貼淺色面磚，並配合精緻典雅之洗石子浮雕裝飾，展現當時富商的氣派。室內樓梯、二樓天花板皆為檜木，並有精美的大理石壁爐，目前皆保存良好。

Above: A general view of the Gu Family Mansion（辜宅外觀）（上圖）

Below: The fireplace of the Gu Family Mansion is ingenuously made with Ionic pillars on the both sides（兩側使用愛奧尼克柱的精美辜宅壁爐）（下圖）

11. Dadaocheng Presbyterian Church （Dadaocheng Chapel）
台灣基督長老教會 （大稻埕禮拜堂）

Completion Year / 1915
創建年代 / 日大正四年

Class / Municipal　　**Category** / Church
級別 / 市定　　類別 / 教堂

Address / No.40, Ganzhou St., Datong District, Taipei City 103
地址 / 台北市大同區甘州街40號

Tel / 02-2553-9741

This church was constructed on the land donated by Lee Chun-sheng, a well-known tea merchant in the late Qing Dynasty, as well as a philosopher rarely seen in the contemporary elite society of Taiwan. Lee's thoughts and published views, which revealed a combination of Christian and Confucius influences, was also a rarity in that time.

Located in the old town area of Dadaocheng, this 2-story Presbyterian church, taller than an ordinary house, is built of red bricks produced in Qing Shui of Taichung, with its façade tastefully decorated with Chinese and Western artistic features. Constructed in a time when people were generally conservative, the church had seats divided into 2 sections and 2 entrance doors for its male and female members. This design, combined with other architectural features, served as an indicator of the context in which the Presbyterian Church was built in the late 19th century and early 20th century. Although the main structure of the church was modelled on the Western ones, the patterns formed with washed terrazzo on its façade drew inspiration from Taiwanese cultural tradition. Its mixture of Taiwanese and Western styles stood out from among contemporary architectures in Taiwan.

　　本教堂由清末知名茶商李春生捐地獻建，李氏亦爲當時一代哲人，在清末台灣士紳社會中所罕見，其論述一方面結合基督教思想，又內含傳統儒家思想，在其年代實屬難得。

　　教堂坐落於大稻埕老市區，挑高二層樓建物以清水紅磚爲其主結構，立面佐以中西特色之藝術裝飾。當時民風保守，禮拜堂男女分坐，並各由左、右入口進出，種種特徵事蹟，見證了19世紀末迄20世紀初年，台北地區基督教發展過程。此建築樣式雖模仿西方教堂，但立面洗石子裝飾仍以台灣傳統圖案出現，融匯了中西風格，在台灣近代建築中誠屬少見。

Above: The arched window located in the middle of the Dadaocheng Presbyterian Church（台灣基督長老教會中央的拱窗）（上圖）

Below: The entrance to the Dadaocheng Presbyterian Church（台灣基督長老教會入口）（下圖）

12. Chen Tian-lai Residence 陳天來故居

Completion Year / around 1920
創建年代 / 1920年代

Class / Municipal **Category** / Residence
級別 / 市定 **類別** / 宅第

Address / No.73, Guide St., Datong District, Taipei City 103
地址 / 台北市大同區貴德街73號

This residence was first built by Chen Tian-lai, a famous figure who played a key role in the development of Taipei's tea industry. The Chen clan, from which large number of talented people were coming forward, had been a leading exponent in the political, trade/economic, and cultural history of contemporary Taiwan. This building was a masterpiece of and a witness to the prime of the Chen's business. With its modern style featuring the diversity of Taiwan in 1920s, this classic structure, built of excellent materials and decorated in detail with exquisite arts, is of immense value of architectural aesthetics.

Ornamentaed with shaped mirrors and woodworks, the reception room on the second floor is rich in aesthetic value. （使用鏡面與講究木工裝飾的二樓會客室，深具建築美學價值。＊）

With its floor plan for spatial function reflecting the life and culture of tea merchants then, the house is a typical example of upper class dwelling. Not only is it a historical place of gathering and banqueting for tea tycoons and dignitaries in the heyday of Da Dao Cheng; it's also a landmark which has written the history of the development of Taipei's tea industry, Guide Street's tea trading firms, and Taipei's architecture.

Above: The back courtyard and building of Chen Tian-lai Residence（陳天來故居後方的庭院與建築外貌 ＊）（上圖）

Above Right: The façade of Chen Tian-lai residence（陳天來故居正面外觀一景 ＊）（右圖上）

Below 2 pictures: The residence has staircases on both sides of the hallway, leading to the second floor. The picture shows the delicate engravings on the stair railings.（大門門廳內左右各有樓梯通往二樓，圖為樓梯扶手精緻的雕工。＊）（下兩圖）

　　本宅創建者陳天來爲台北茶葉發展過程中重要人物，且陳氏家族人才輩出，在近代台灣政治、經貿及文化史上有代表性地位，此建物爲其事業高峰之傑作與重要見證。本建築展現1920年代台灣多元特色之近代建築風格，建材優良、精緻之細部裝修工藝爲經典之作，深具建築美學價值。空間功能配置反映茶商當時生活文化，爲典型上層商人住屋之代表。此建物爲大稻埕全盛時代茶商名人聚集宴客的歷史地點，且作爲台北茶葉發展史、貴德街茶行史及台北建築史之重要紀錄。

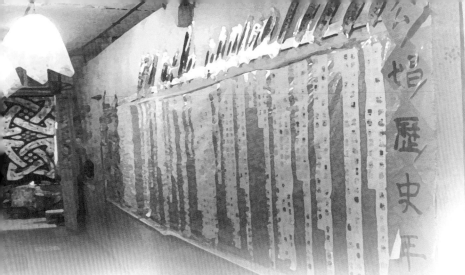

13. Uen Meng Building on Guisui Street　歸綏街文萌樓

Completion Year / around 1930
創建年代 / 1930年代

Class / Municipal
級別 / 市定

Category / Industrial Facilities
類別 / 產業設施

Address / No.139, Gueisuei St., Datong District, Taipei City 103
地址 / 台北市大同區歸綏街139號

A general view of Uen Meng Building
（文萌樓外觀現貌 * ）

A typical example of the store house in the colonial time of 1940s, this solid structure, still in good shape covered with yellow-green tile in national defense or anti-raid color, features its Baroque style imported by the Japanese from Europe. After Taiwan's restoration in 1947 to the ROC, this building began being used for a public-run whorehouse, a location which brings back historical memories of Taipei's urban area development as well as its river-port sex business. It is also a particularly memorable place, because a campaign began at this spot vehemently opposing the official abolishment of public whorehouses. The indoor compartment or layout of this well-preserved house also reflects the spatial needs and functions of the early-time sex business with the particular atmosphere of a public whorehouse still emanating.

Above: The entrance hall of Uen Meng Building（文萌樓大門入口一景＊）（上圖）

Below: The interior of Uen Meng Building. The signboard hanging on the wall of the hallway is one that was hung on the entrance gate. Small rooms line the hallway.（文萌樓室內現貌，走道上方的招牌為當年掛在大門外的舊物，走道兩側為小房室。＊）（下圖）

　　為殖民時期1940年代店屋類型，日人移植歐洲巴洛克建築元素，覆以黃綠色國防色磁磚，建築物實質條件尚佳。光復後，1947年始為公娼館所在，為都市發展史河港城市性產業歷史記憶地區，亦是反廢娼運動中心，尤具紀念意義。建築物室內隔間亦反映出當時產業的空間要求，仍維持公娼館氣氛，相當完整。

14. Dadaocheng Qianqiu Street Stores 大稻埕千秋街店屋

Completion Year / Late Qing to Early Japanese Colonial Period
創建年代 / 清末、日治初期之間

Class / Municipal   **Category** / Old Market Street
級別 / 市定   類別 / 古市街

Address / No.51 and No.53, Guide St., Datong District, Taipei City 103
地址 / 台北市大同區貴德街51及53號

In the Dadaocheng port area, there used to be blocks of planned buildings located within the market and store streets (also known as Qingqiu Street), as part of the then Qing Court Governor Liu Ming-chuan's new policy. Those buildings, judging from their history and features of the materials used, belong to the architecture and style found between the last years of the Qing Dynasty and early years of the Japanese reign, evidenced by the early-time thriving of the Tamsui River area. It, thus, displayed the characteristics of "Houses Street" occupied by foreign business firms and rich tea merchants.

The stores and houses, built along the old street close to the Tam Shui River, must elevate the foundations of their arcade houses by 3 feet to avoid floods and to facilitate walking and delivery of goods. Today these elevated foundations are a special feature of buildings on this street – that is rarely seen elsewhere in Taipei. The buildings which are used for opening groceries in Japanese time are a feature of Taiwan's earliest commercial culture. In this neighborhood, historical and cultural relics abound along with a wealth of humanities and anecdotes.

劉銘傳新政時期在大稻埕港區所規劃市街（千秋街）之相關建築，依歷史及建材特色推論，爲清末日治初期之建物，見證台北早期淡水河運繁榮，呈現出洋行茶商聚集之街屋特色。

建物沿古街，爲防水患與方便卸貨，騎樓提高三尺，爲北市罕見之特色。建物在日治時期開雜貨店，具早期商業文化之特色。本區周邊多爲歷史文化遺跡，並蘊藏了豐富的人文軼事。

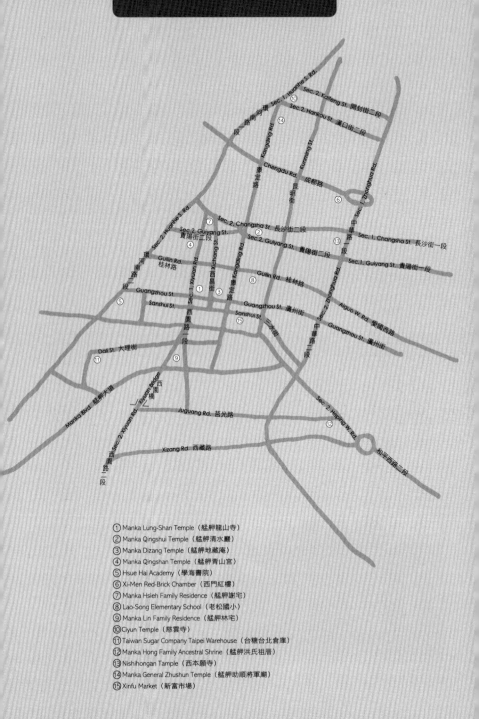

Wanhua

（行政區 / 台北市萬華區）
District

① Manka Lung-Shan Temple （艋舺龍山寺）

② Manka Qingshui Temple （艋舺清水巖）

③ Manka Dizang Temple （艋舺地藏庵）

④ Manka Qingshan Temple （艋舺青山宮）

⑤ Hsue Hai Academy （學海書院）

⑥ Xi-Men Red-Brick Chamber （西門紅樓）

⑦ Manka Hsieh Family Residence （艋舺謝宅）

⑧ Lao-Song Elementary School （老松國小）

⑨ Manka Lin Family Residence （艋舺林宅）

⑩ Ciyun Temple （慈雲寺）

⑪ Taiwan Sugar Company Taipei Warehouse （台糖台北倉庫）

⑫ Manka Hong Family Ancestral Shrine （艋舺洪氏祖厝）

⑬ Nishihongan Tample （西本願寺）

⑭ Manka General Zhushun Temple （艋舺助順將軍廟）

⑮ Xinfu Market （新富市場）

Wanhua （行政區 / 台北市萬華區）

1. Manka Lung-Shan Temple　艋舺龍山寺

Completion Year / 1738
創建年代 / 清乾隆三年

Class / 2　　　　　**Category** / Temple
級別 / 第二級　　　　類別 / 祠廟

Address / No.211, Guangzhou St., Wanhua District, Taipei City 108
地址 / 台北市萬華區廣州街211號

Tel / 02-2302-5162

As the hub of religion, self-governing and self-defending in the Manka area, this temple was founded in the 3rd year of the Qian Long period of the Qing Dynasty (1783). The 260-year old Lung-Shan Temple, Taiwan's premier ancient temple is devoted to the Goddess of Mercy, a branch temple with a split spirit brought to Taiwan by immigrants from Jin Jiang, Nan An and Hui An from the Long-Shan Temple at An Hai Village of Jin Jiang in Fu Jian. Today's Temple size and shape is based on the renovations done in the 9th year of Japanese Emperor O-sho (1920) by a famous Quan Zhou carpenter named Wang Yi Shun. This temple is rich in exquisite bronze, stone, and wood carvings, in particular, the octagon caisson ceiling in the front hall, the bell and drum towers, sedan-type roof ridge, and the circular caisson ceiling in the main hall – they are all incomparably superb and splendid.

The main gate of Manka Lung-Shan Temple
（龍山寺正門一景＊）

The temple was designated as the 2nd grade of Historical Site as National Shrine and Temple on August 19 in the 74th year of the ROC on Taiwan (1985). Overall, the architecture of this temple is splendid and magnificent, clearly under a strict and meticulous construction by using the best quality stones from Quan Zhou. It has become a platform for a variety of craftsmen and art masters to display their skills and talents. Throughout the year, numerous worshipers, followers and visitors, home and abroad, are flocking in, making it a world-famous tourist attraction.

Above: The interior of Manka Lung-Shan Temple
（龍山寺內景）（上圖）

Below: A bird's eye view of Manka Lung-Shan Temple
（龍山寺鳥瞰）（下圖）

　　本寺創建於清乾隆三年（1738），為艋舺地區之信仰、自治與自衛中心。供奉觀世音菩薩，係晉江、南安、惠安三邑籍居民從晉江安海鄉龍山寺分靈來台者。今寺規制係日大正九年（1920）修建者，由泉州名匠王益順主持，前殿八角藻井、鐘鼓樓轎式屋頂及正殿圓形藻井，皆精美絕倫。

　　民國七十四年（1985）八月十九日，指定為國定祠廟第二級古蹟。綜觀此寺建築施工嚴謹，雕刻精密而考究，多用泉州質地精良的石材，其豪華壯麗，美不勝收，成為工匠藝師展現藝術才華的殿堂。龍山寺經年香火鼎盛、熱鬧非常，同時也是國外觀光客樂於參訪的著名地點。

2. Manka Qingshui Temple (Zu Shi Temple)
艋舺清水巖（祖師廟）

Completion Year / 1787
創建年代 / 清乾隆五十二年

Class / 3　　　　Category / Temple
級別 / 第三級　　　類別 / 祠廟

Address / No.81, Kangding Rd., Wanhua District, Taipei City 108
地址 / 台北市萬華區康定路81號

Tel / 02-2371-1517

The inscribed board on the entrance gate of Manka Qingshui Temple（艋舺清水巖匾額＊）

Qingshui Temple, also commonly known as Zu Shi Temple, was founded in the 52nd year of the Qian Long period of the Qing Dynasty (1787) The Divine Progenitor Qing Shui, a guardian of the people of An Xi from Fu Jian. Worshipped as the head god, the deification of the high monk Chen Chao-ying of the Song Dynasty, he has been long revered for his lifetime devotion to giving medical care for the masses and for praying for rain in times of drought. In the 3rd year of Xian Fong period of the Qing Dynasty, armed flights coming from ethnic conflicts broke out at Ding Xia in the

Manka area, resulting in the burnt-down of the temple. It was not rebuilt until the 6th year of the Tong Zhi period of the Qing Dynasty (1867). The present architecture is what it originally was with 3 halls; now the structure of the temple contains 3 row-houses with 2 entrance and 2 corridors, where one can enjoy the marvelously simple carvings on its stone walls and beams and around its dragon pillars, along with the superb tile carvings on the corridor walls.

創建於清乾隆五十二年（1787），俗稱祖師廟，主祀清水祖師，爲安溪人的守護神，乃爲福建安溪縣移民自該縣湖內鄉清水巖分靈而來者。咸豐三年（1853）艋舺發生「頂下郊拚」械鬥事件時，因三邑人借道攻打同安人而被焚毀，至同治六年（1867）方重建。原有三殿，後殿毀後未建，今爲三開間兩進兩廊兩護龍的殿宇建築，但保有清代古樸的風貌。

Top: The façade of Manka Qingshui Temple（艋舺清水巖正面外觀＊）（上圖）

Above: The interior of Manka Qingshui Temple（艋舺清水巖內景＊）（中圖）

Below: A bird's eye view on Manka Qingshui Temple（艋舺清水巖鳥瞰）（下圖）

3. Manka Dizang Temple (Manka Temple of King Earth Treasure)
艋舺地藏庵（地藏王廟）

Completion Year / 1760
創建年代 / 清乾隆二十五年

Class / 3
級別 / 第三級

Category / Temple
類別 / 祠廟

Address / No.245, Xichang St., Wanhua District, Taipei City 108
地址 / 台北市萬華區西昌街245號

Tel / 02-1306-6352

The statue of Dizang is worshiped in Manka Dizang Temple（艋舺地藏庵供奉之地藏王像 ＊）

This convent temple, founded in the 25th year of the Qian Long period of the Qing Dynasty (1760) and renovated in the 18th year of the Dao Guang period of the Qing Dynasty (1838), is dedicated to the worshiping of King Dizang, literally meaning "Earth Treasury or Earth Womb," who is popularly regarded and respected as the guardian of the earth, one of the 8 Dhyani-Bodhisattvas. In the ancient times of repeated natural disasters and man-made misfortunes frequented, King Dizang, with her sole duty to escort the souls of the deceased to the nirvana, was popularly respected as a priority god to pray for. This temple is a 3-row-house architecture with a single hall entrance in a well-preserved traditional single hall style, it is perfectly retained as a mid-Qing Dynasty temple. It looks simple and plain with a brief and succinct swallowtail roof ridge, let alone those simple and unadorned carving decorations.

本寺創建於清乾隆二十五年（1760），道光十八年（1838）重修。主祀地藏王菩薩，又稱地藏王廟，早年在天災人禍頻傳的時代，引領亡靈的地藏王菩薩，很受民間重視，也相當興盛。本寺為三開間單進之獨立建築，迄今仍保持清代中葉單殿式寺廟建築的風格。建築形貌簡樸，屋頂採用簡潔的燕尾翹脊，雕飾有樸拙之風。

4. Manka Qingshan Temple   艋舺青山宮

Completion Year / 1856
創建年代 / 清咸豐六年

Class / 3   **Category** / Temple
級別 / 第三級   **類別** / 祠廟

Address / No.218, Sec. 2, Guiyang St., Wanhua District, Taipei City 108
地址 / 台北市萬華區貴陽街二段218號

Tel / 02-2382-2296

Manka Qingshan Temple, a temple dedicated to the deified spirit of Zhang Gun, Honorable King of Ling An, was first founded in the 6th year of the Xian Fong period of the Qing Dynasty (1856), two years after a fisherman of Hui An, Fu Jian,

The façade of Manka Qingshan Temple
（艋舺青山宮外觀 * ）

proposing to set up the branch out of his hometown's Qingshan Temple. The architecture consists of three rows of houses with three entrances, with two corridors to connect on either side. The present look is a result of renovations made in the 13th year of Emperor Showa (1938). Inside, one is immediately attracted by the temple's grand carved stone beams, where granite and Qing Dou stone are mainly used, and wall paintings with incomparable handicraft. In front of the main hall, the stone column, pillars and piling stones are retrieved from the materials left when the Yuan Shan Shito Shrine was torn town.

Above: The awesomely illuminated interior of Manka Qingshan Temple
（艋舺青山宮內景金碧輝煌＊）
（上圖）

Below: The beautiful eight side caisson ceiling in Manka Qingshan Temple
（艋舺青山宮內漂亮的八角藻井＊）
（下圖）

創建於清咸豐六年（1856），供奉靈安尊王張滾，清咸豐四年（1854）福建惠安籍漁民自其故鄉青山廟奉請而來。廟宇為三開間三進兩廊的建築，今貌乃昭和十三年（1938）重修者，入口正面以石雕為主，花崗石與青斗石並用，前殿的石柱與石垛，乃使用圓山神舍所遺之石材。

5. Hsue Hai Academy（Now Kao Family Ancestral Shrine）
學海書院（今高氏宗祠）

Completion Year / 1837
創建年代 / 清道光十七年

Class / 3   **Category** / Private Academy
級別 / 第三級   **類別** / 書院

Address / No.93, Sec. 2, Huanhe S. Rd., Wanhua District, Taipei City 108
地址 / 台北市萬華區環河南路二段93號

In Taipei, Hsue Hai Academy is the only remainder of an ancient academy or educational institute of its category. This institute, originally named "Wen Jia," an euphemism for the relatively vulgar name of "Wanka," was initiated by the then Tamsui County Magistrate Lou Yun in the 17th year of the Dao Guang period of the Qing Dynasty (1837). There is an inscription bearing the new name of "Hsue Hai or Learning Seas Academy" granted by Liu Yun-ke, the then Qing Court Governor General of Fu Jian and Zhe Jiang, who paid a visit proposing the name change. Today it serves as the ancestral shrine of the Gao's family who purchased the estate under the Japanese rule; but in recent years, the broadening of Huanhe South Road has eroded the space of entrance and main hall, both of which were newly built. The front hall served as a classroom and the center of the academy; in the rear is the ceremonial hall, and the wings on both sides were dormitories. Also, with a Zhu Xi Shrine, the academy was an important link in the traditional Chinese education system; it was the forerunner of today's academic education, providing a place for worship and residence as well as learning. Teachers and students alike lived in the academy.

學海書院係台北市僅存的書院古蹟，創建於清光道十七年（1837），由淡水廳同知婁雲發起興建。原名為「文甲」，為「艋舺」雅稱，閩浙總督劉韻珂

Above Left: The flag stones in the front courtyeard of Hsue Hai Academy have been erected for decades. （學海書院前庭立著的夾杆石為昔日舊物 ＊ ）（左上圖）

Above Right: The images of Door Gods on the entrance door of Hsue Hai Academy （學海書院的門神 ＊ ）（右上圖）

Below: The current state of the main gate of Hsue Hai Academy （學海書院正門今貌 ＊ ）（下圖）

巡視台灣，易名學海，並題額曰學海書院。日治時期高姓族人購為宗祠，但近年環河南路拓寬，門廳乃退縮新建。空間佈置係以講堂為中心向外延伸，左右對稱，配置講堂、朱子祠、學舍。

6. Xi-Men Red-Brick Chamber (Now Red Chamber Theater)
西門紅樓（今紅樓劇場）

Completion Year / 1908
創建年代 / 日明治四十一年

Class / 3
級別 / 第三級

Category / Other
類別 / 其他

Address / No.10, Chengdu Rd., Wanhua District, Taipei City 108
地址 / 台北市萬華區成都路10號

Tel / 02-2311-9380

The site of this brick-made structure once housed the first wood-built government-run market in the first years of the Japanese colonial rule. At present, the location of a mini theater called Hong Lou Ju Chang or Red Chamber Theater, this building was initiated in the 41st year of Emperor Mei Ji (1908). Rebuilt from its market site into a 2-story brick house; it then became a western-style, octagonal architecture based on a "cross-shape" plan, whose design was prepared by Mr. Kinto Zuro, then working for the Division of Constructions & Repairs of

The extraordinary beauty of the Xi-Men Red-brick Chamber in the light at night（夜晚的西門紅樓在燈光下美麗異常）

Above: The roof truss structure of top floor of Xi-Men Red-Brick Chamber（西門紅樓頂層屋架結構）（上圖）

Above Left: A close view of the Xi-Men Red-Brick Chamber（西門紅樓外貌近觀）（左頁上圖）

Below Left: The interior of the Red Chamber Theatre, the former Xi-Men Red-Brick Chamber（改為紅樓劇場後的內部一景）（左頁下圖）

the Office of Taiwan Governor General. It features brick-laid walls, steel and RC floors and a steel trussing girder roof, radiating out from the hub in different directions like an umbrella rib. The theater presents and promotes a variety of talk shows, and singing and performing art activities.

　　創建於明治四十一年（1908），原為日治初期台灣第一座官建木造市場，後改建為紅磚造的八角形與十字形二樓洋式建築，由總督府營繕課近藤十郎設計。牆樓為紅磚砌成，樓版為鋼筋水泥，屋頂為鋼骨桁架，有如雨傘骨般呈放射狀，非常具有特色。西門紅樓今已改為劇場，以演出及推廣說唱藝術等各類型的藝文展演活動為主。

7. Manka Hsieh Family Residence　艋舺謝宅

Completion Year / 1799
創建年代 / 清嘉慶四年

Class / Municipal　　　**Category** / Residence
級別 / 市定　　　　　　**類別** / 宅第

Address / No.88, Xichang St., Wanhua District, Taipei City 108
地址 / 台北市萬華區西昌街88號

Manka Hsieh Family Residence was originally a trading office building dealing with business transactions between Taipei and the cities of mainland China, mainly Zhang Zhou and Quan Zhou. It had historically contributed a great deal to the commercial development of the Manka area. The mansion is a quadrangle architecture--a traditional Chinese residential compound with houses around a courtyard. This 2-story brick-made town house turned into a hotel named Xing Guang or Star Light Hotel. This simple and plain street row house, unadorned, epitomizes the traditional presence of an earlier-time inn wedged into downtown bustling noise.

Above: Manka Hsieh Family Residence before it was refurbished（艋舺謝宅整修前之舊觀）（上圖）

Left: The latticed window of the main hall of Manka Hsieh Family Residence（艋舺謝宅正廳的格扇）（左頁圖）

艋舺謝宅原為郊行，掌握台北與漳泉之貿易，對艋舺歷史發展有不少貢獻。是一座四合院宅第。日治後期改為星光旅社，整建為二層樓的磚造臨街建築，一樓拱廊、二樓長形窗，設有騎樓，柱子使用磚砌，樓板為木樑支撐，唯中庭門廳乃維持原貌。這棟平實的街屋代表著早期鬧市裡傳統客棧的一種類型。

The entrance to Xing Guang (Star Light) Hotel（星光旅社正門一景）

8. Lao-Song Elementary School 老松國小

Completion Year / 1896
創建年代 / 日明治二十九年

Class / Municipal
級別 / 市定

Category / Other
類別 / 其他

Address / No.64, Guilin Rd., Wanhua District, Taipei City 108
地址 / 台北市萬華區桂林路64號

Tel / 02-2336-1266

One of the earliest elementary schools established in the first years of the Japanese colonial rule, Lao-Song Elementary School was founded in the 29th year of Emperor Mei Ji period (1896). In February of the 44th year of the Republic of China on Taiwan (1955), the façade of the main campus structure was expanded to become a 3-story steel and RC building. The semi-circular corridors, which go along the campus buildings, give an intriguingly classic taste – display a stereotype early-time elementary school which is worth preserving as a historical site. Since its inception, the school has produced numerous talents in the Manka area, playing a significant role in the development of national education in Taipei City.

A long corridor outside of the classrooms of Lao-Song Elementary School（老松國小內教室外長廊＊）

創立於日明治二十九年（1896），原爲日治初期台灣最早的一批小學。民國四十四年（1955）年二月，正面校舍（本棟）添建爲三層鋼筋水泥大樓。校舍走廊爲半圓栱式，帶有一絲古典趣味，爲早期小學校舍之典型，值得保存。老松國小自創建以來，培育造就了無數艋舺地區優秀人才，在台北市教育史上具很大意義。

Right: A path near the inner side of main gate of Lao-Song Elementary School（老松國小大門內側旁的小徑＊）（上圖）

Below: The school buildings and large sports field of Lao-Song Elementary School（老松國小校舍及大操場＊）（下圖）

9. Manka Lin Family Residence (Wanhua Lin Family Residence)
艋舺林宅 (萬華林宅)

Completion Year / 1932
創建年代 / 日昭和六年

Class / Municipal
級別 / 市定

Category / Residence
類別 / 宅第

Address / No.24 and No.26, Lane 306, Sec. 1, Xiyuan Rd., Wanhua District, Taipei City 108
地址 / 台北市萬華區西園路一段306巷24、26號

This 3-story, steel and RC residence building was built by the Lin's family, a local distinguished family. The layout of the structure is irregularly shaped with three façades facing the highways, thus looking conspicuous from a distance. The entrance is contained in an arcade house with the design and pattern of the main gate and the windows on either side being perfectly symmetrical. A rooftop platform affords a good commanding to enjoy a distant view. The chiefly Chinese style interior of the mansion making this site Taipei's remainder of a representative civilian house of 1930s in Taipei.

A general view of Manka Lin Family Residence
(萬華林宅外觀一景＊)

　　此宅第爲當地望族富戶林氏所建，爲三層鋼筋混凝土建築。這座三層樓華
宅的平面呈不規則形狀，三邊臨馬路，因此外觀甚爲突出。入口設騎樓，大門
及左右窗對稱，屋頂上設平台可供遠眺，室內裝修以中國風格爲主，是台北新
現存1930年代民間巨宅之代表作。

10. Ciyun Temple　慈雲寺

Completion Year / 1924
創建年代 / 日大正十三年

Class / Municipal　**Category** / Temple
級別 / 市定　類別 / 祠廟

Address / No.119 , No.121 and No.123, Lane 306, Sec. 2, Hankou St., Wanhua District, Taipei City 108
地址 / 台北市萬華區漢口街二段119、121、123號

Devoted to the worshiping of Goddess of Mercy or Guan-yin as the host image, this Buddhism temple was built under the Japanese colonial rule, utilizing the new land in the urban area beyond the West Gate gained after the landfill project was completed. The construction funds were donated by a Mr. Chang to establish it a Buddhism Temple exclusively for fasting or vegetarian-dieting. The main body of this temple is a brick structure completed in the Emperor O-sho years with its floor constructed with H-shape steel beams. In front of the temple, there are brick-made arch corridors which look like a worship pavilion. The second floor housing is entirely made of wood. A tablet altar is installed in the main hall, on either side of which, there are some chambers and units for living or work space – a featured harmonious combination of temple and residence.

　　本寺為日治時期西門外填地計畫之後興建的佛寺，主祀觀世音菩薩。為張氏籌資建造，是一座齋堂式佛寺。建築主體部分為日大正年間紅磚之構造，樓板使用工字鋼樑，寺前設置紅磚拱廊，有如拜亭，二樓則全為傳統的木結構。除了明間的神龕以外，左右還留設一些房間，可說是將寺廟與住宅巧妙地結合起來，頗具特色。

11. Taiwan Sugar Company Taipei Warehouse
台糖台北倉庫

Completion Year / 1909
創建年代 / 日明治四十二年

Class / Municipal
級別 / 市定

Category / Other
類別 / 其他

Address / No.132-7, No.132-9 and No.132-10, Dali St., Wanhua District, Taipei City 108
地址 / 台北市萬華區大理街132號之7、之9、之10

This warehouse witnessed all the developments and changes taking place of Taiwan's sugar making industry in the Taipei basin from the Qing Dynasty to the Japanese ruling time. The only sugar factory in northern Taiwan beyond Taoyuan, the name of this neighborhood, to this date, is still commonly known as Tang Kuo Li or Sugar-place. Among the many architectural features of this warehouse are its trussing system, trussed girder, pole and span as well as brick arch gate – all are the typical techniques and practices found in 1910s. In front of the warehouse, noteworthy is the well-preserved platform for the early-time mini sugar train to stop or call.

The old platform preserved in the Taiwan Sugar Company Taipei Warehouse（台糖台北倉庫內保留的舊月台）

此座倉庫為清代及日治時期台北盆地蔗糖工業的一項見證，其地名仍為糖廍里，為桃園以北唯一的糖廠。此倉庫的建築具有多方面特色，其木桁架及紅磚拱門皆屬1910年代之典型作法，加上倉庫前方仍保存早期小火車停靠之月台，十分特別。

A bird's eye view of the Taiwan Sugar Company Taipei Warehouse（台糖台北倉庫鳥瞰）

A general view of the Taiwan Sugar Company Taipei Warehouse（台糖台北倉庫外觀一景＊）

12. Manka Hong Family Ancestral Shrine　艋舺洪氏祖厝

Completion Year / Qing Dynasty Daoguang Years
創建年代 / 清道光年間

Class / Municipal
級別 / 市定

Category / Residence
類別 / 宅第

Address / No.1, No.3 and No.5, Lane 112, Juguang Rd., Wanhua District, Taipei City 108
　　　　　No.2, No.6, No.8 and No.10, Alley 8, Lane 112, Juguang Rd., Wanhua District, Taipei City 108
地址 / 台北市萬華區莒光路112巷1.3.5號,112巷9弄2.6.8.10號

The interior of Manka Hong Family Ancestral Shrine
（艋舺洪氏祖厝內部陳設一景）

This age-old and antique shrine, the largest-scale of its category and a historical rarity in Taipei, was built during the Dao Guang period of the Qing Dynasty. The whole architecture comprises three rows of house structures, guarded by single wings and corridors; the construction materials it used were diversified with particular attention paid to its superb and splendid wood carvings. Inside the house exhibited are all the artifacts and relics, such as ancient desks and tables, age-old well – all are worth looking at and preserving. The overall building occupies a well-knit neighborhood, forming an integral part of the cultural value it represents.

本建物約建於清道光
年間，年代久遠，建築規
模宏大，為台北少見的宅
第。其建築為三進帶單邊
護龍的格局，建材多樣，
木雕也精美講究。而室內
文物如供桌、古井，亦具
保存價值。整體建物所形
成之區域完整，易彰顯其
文化價值。

Above：A general view of Manka
Hong Family Ancestral Shrine（艋舺
洪氏祖厝外觀一景）（上圖）

Right：The old well in Manka Hong
Family Ancestral Shrine（艋舺洪氏
祖厝內的古井）（下圖）

13. Nishihongan Temple (Including Bell Tower and Jushin Hall)
西本願寺（鐘樓、樹心會館）

Completion Year / 1923
創建年代 / 日大正十二年

Class / Municipal   **Category** / Other
級別 / 市定   **類別** / 其他

Address / Sec. 1, Zhonghua Rd., Wanhua District, Taipei City 108 (between Sec.2, Changsha St. and Sec.2 Guiyang St.)
地址 / 台北市萬華區中華路1段（長沙街2段與貴陽街2段間）

During the Japanese colonial period, this Zen Temple was the largest Japanese Buddhist Temple in Taipei and around Taiwan. As one of the representative religious architectures at that time, it, as well as Higashihogan Temple and Huguo Chan Buddhist Temple of the Linji School, have played a significant role in the historical and academic development of the religion in Taiwan. The bell tower of the temple, which was completed in 1923, was characterized by wood mortise and tenon crafts such as the grand bucket arch (Dou Gong). Shu Xin (Tree Heart) Clubhouse, inauguarted in the same year, assumed the exquisitely elegant style of the classic brick architecture of the late O-sho period, and had slightly expanded its structure in the 1930s.

本寺為日治時期當時台北乃至台灣最大之日式佛寺，與東本願寺、臨濟護國禪寺等同為當時重要佛寺之建築代表，具有歷史及宗教學術上之意義。鐘樓與於1923年落成，雄碩斗拱等木結構為其特色。樹心會館同年完成，有大正末期紅磚建築的精緻典雅特色，1930年代之後略有增建。

14. Manka General Zhushun Temple（Jinde Temple）
艋舺助順將軍廟（晉德宮）

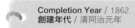

Completion Year / 1862
創建年代 / 清同治元年

Class / Municipal   **Category** / Temple
級別 / 市定   **類別** / 祠廟

Address / No.13, Kangding Rd., Wanhua District, Taipei City 108
地址 / 台北市萬華區康定路13號

Jinde Temple, always known as "General Temple," was first built in the 1st year of the Tong Zhi period of the Qing Dynasty, followed by intermittent renovations and repairs, giving its carvings and architecture a relatively high historical significance. This General Temple is dedicated to a god worshiped by port laborers and ship dock workers and so the presence of such a relic witnesses the historical development of this locality from a booming port to a bustling market. It is a rarity to see as there are only two of their kind remaining in Taipei area.

The interior of Manka General Zhushun Temple
（艋舺助順將軍廟內一景＊）

Above: The apearance of Manka General Zhushun Temple（艋舺助順將軍廟外觀＊）（上圖）

Left: In front of Manka General Zhushun Temple（艋舺助順將軍廟門前一景＊）（下圖）

晉德宮又稱為「將軍廟」，初建於同治元年，其後雖陸續修建，雕刻、結構仍具一定歷史價值。將軍廟是船頭勞工祭拜之神，本廟見證地方發展歷史，台北地區僅有二處，具稀少性。

15. Xinfu Market　新富市場（本館、辦公處、宿舍）

Completion Year / around 1920
創建年代 / 日大正年間

Class / Municipal　　　**Category** / Industrial Facilities
級別 / 市定　　　　　　**類別** / 產業設施

Address / No.70, Sanshui St., Wanhua District, Taipei City 108
地址 / 台北市萬華區三水街70號

Tel / 02-2302-1673

This building of profound historical significance is one of the remaining few markets built in Taipei during the Japanese colonial period. Being U-shaped, Xinfu Market is a circled structure in which people may move smoothly, with one side facing the patio in the center of the market which assisits in lighting and ventilation. The curves and turns on the outer walls of the market, being highly decorative, resemble those on the contemporary avant-garde architecture. The main body of the market, while maintaining its general layout, was later added with a wooden office and living quarters. The integration of office and dormitory is distinguished in its own right.

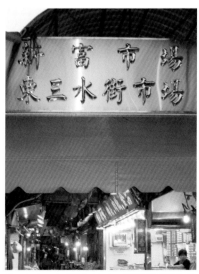

The signboard of Xinfu Market（新富市場現今招牌）

The entrance to the office of the Xinfu Market（新富市場辦公處入口外觀）

本建物為台北市日治時期建置且至今仍留存的少數市場之一，具有歷史價值。市場平面為馬蹄形，中間留設採光通風天井，可繞室內一圈，動線流暢，且市場外飾線具裝飾性風格，屬當代建築前衛作法。除市場本館外，並附設木造的辦公處及住宿空間，且主結構仍維持原格局、原物料，另辦公與管理宿舍空間結合，具特殊建築類型特色。

Being U-shaped, the Xinfu Market has a patio which assists in lighting and ventilation.（新富市場平面為馬蹄形，中間留採光通風天井＊）

撫遠街 Fuyuan St.

Sec. 6, Nanjing E. Rd. 南京東路六段

Sec. 5, Nanjing E. Rd. 南京東路五段

Sec. 3, Nangang Rd. 南港路三段

Raohe St. 饒河街

Sec. 1, Keelung Rd. 基隆路一段

虎林街 Hulin St.

Songlong Rd. 松隆路

Zhongpo N. Rd. 中坡北路

① Songshan Market（松山市場）

Songshan (行政區 / 台北市松山區)

1. Songshan Market　松山市場

Completion Year / 1909
創建年代 / 日明治四十二年

Class / Municipal
級別 / 市定

Category / Industrial Facilities
類別 / 產業設施

Address / No.679, Sec. 4, Bade Rd., Songshan District, Taipei City 105
地址 / 台北市松山區八德路四段679號

The Songshan Market attributed its rise to the business boom resulting from water transport as a former hub of commodity transaction. The market began being forming as early as the Qing Dynasty until the market place was first built in 1909; and it continues to this date for nearly 100 years. The market plays a profoundly significant role in fostering the development of Xikou River Port. To date, the structure, on a whole, still preserves the original look with its cypress truss girders and outer cobbled walls remaining in a fairly good shape.

The signboard and office of the Songshan Market（松山市場現今招牌及辦公室）

● The photographs with * marks are offered by Artist Publishing Co.
（本書圖說後有 * 符號者，為藝術家出版社拍攝）

The well-functioned red wood purlin in the Songshan Market（松山市場內現狀良好的檜木桁架）

松山市場的興起，係因水運而使商業活動興盛，曾是物流集散中樞。自清代起就逐漸形成市集，直至1909年興建松山市場延續至今，已近百年之久，見證錫口河港發展歷程，深具歷史意義。至今，其建物大致仍保有原有形貌，檜木桁架及洗石子外牆保存狀況尚佳。

The outer walls of facial washed terrazzos in the Songshan Market（松山市場洗石子外牆現貌）

A List of Historical Sites in Taipei
台 北 市 古 蹟 一 覽 表

Number 序號	Class 級別	Name 標的物	Date 公告日	District 行政區
1	1	Taipei City Wall-North Gate, East Gate, South Gate, Auxiliary South Gate【台北府城門】	1983.12.28 1998.09.03	Zhong zheng（中正區）
2	2	Qing Dynasty Taiwan Provincial Administration Hall【台灣布政使司衙門】	1985.08.19	Zhong zheng（中正區）
3	3	Huang Family Widow's Memorial【黃氏節孝坊】	1985.08.19	Zhong zheng（中正區）
4	3	Hong Tengyun Memorial【急公好義坊】	1985.08.19	Zhong zheng（中正區）
5	2	Dalongdong Baoan Temple【大龍峒保安宮】	1985.08.19	Datong（大同區）
6	3	Xia Hai Cheng Huang Temple of City God【大稻埕霞海城隍廟】	1985.08.19	Datong（大同區）
7	3	Chen Dexing Ancestral Shrine【陳德星堂】	1985.08.19	Datong（大同區）
8	3	Chen Yueji Ancestral Mansion【陳悅記祖宅】	1985.08.19	Datong（大同區）
9	2	Manka Lung-Shan Temple【艋舺龍山寺】	1985.08.19	Wanhua（萬華區）
10	3	Manka Qingshui Temple【艋舺清水巖】	1985.08.19	Wanhua（萬華區）
11	3	Manka Dizang Temple【艋舺地藏庵】	1985.08.19	Wanhua（萬華區）
12	3	Manka Qingshan Temple【艋舺青山宮】	1985.08.19	Wanhua（萬華區）
13	3	Hsue Hai Academy【學海書院】	1985.08.19	Wanhua（萬華區）
14	3	Zhou Family Widow's Memorial【周氏節孝坊】	1985.08.19	Beitou（北投區）
15	3	Cixian Temple, Shilin【士林慈誠宮】	1985.08.19	Shilin（士林區）
16	3	Huiji Temple, Chih-Shan-Yan【芝山巖惠濟宮】	1985.08.19	Shilin（士林區）
17	3	Chih-Shan-Yen Gate【芝山岩隘門】	1985.08.10	Shilin（士林區）
18	3	Jiying Temple, Jingmei【景美集應廟】	1985.08.19	Wenshan（文山區）
19	1	Yuanshan Prehistoric Site【圓山遺址】	1988.04.25	Zhongshan（中山區）
20	3	Yifang Mansion【義芳居】	1989.08.18	Daan（大安區）
21	3	Original Kangyo Bank Building【勸業銀行舊廈】	1991.05.24	Zhong zheng（中正區）
22	3	Tomb of Lin Xiu-jun【林秀俊墓】	1991.11.23	Neihu（內湖區）
23	2	Taipei Assembly Hall【台北公會堂】	1992.01.10	Zhong zheng（中正區）
24	3	Taipei Confucius Temple【台北孔廟】	1992.01.10	Datong（大同區）
25	3	The Railway Division of Taiwan Governor General's Bureau of Transportation【台灣總督府交通局鐵道部】	1992.01.10	Datong（大同區）
26	3	Taipei Post Office【台北郵局】	1992.08.14	Zhong zheng（中正區）
27	3	Japanese Colonial-era Taipei Water Plant【台北水道水源地】	1993.02.05	Zhong zheng（中正區）
28	3	Original Taiwan Education Association Building【原台灣教育會館】	1993.02.05	Zhong zheng（中正區）
29	2	Chin-Shan-Yen Prehistoric Site【芝山岩遺址】	1993.02.05	Shilin（士林區）
30	3	Xi-Men Red-Brick Chamber【西門紅樓】	1997.02.20	Wanhua（萬華區）
31	3	Beitou Hot Spring Public Bath【北投溫泉浴場】	1997.02.20	Beitou（北投區）
32	3	Former U.S. Ambassador's Residence【前美國大使官邸】	1997.02.20	Zhongshan（中山區）
33	3	Taipei Third Girls' High School【台北第三高女】	1997.02.20	Zhongshan（中山區）
34	Municipal（市定）	Wistaria House【紫藤廬】	1997.07.23	Daan（大安區）

Number 序號	Class 級別	Name 標的物	Date 公告日	District 行政區
35	Municipal (市定)	Treasure Hill Temple【寶藏巖】	1997.08.05	Zhong zheng（中正區）
36	Municipal (市定)	Bell Tower, Donghe Temple【東和禪寺鐘樓】	1997.08.05	Zhong zheng（中正區）
37	Municipal (市定)	Futai Street Mansion【台北撫台街洋樓】	1997.11.21	Zhong zheng（中正區）
38	Municipal (市定)	Original National Taiwan University Hospital【台大醫院舊館】	1998.03.25	Zhong zheng（中正區）
39	Municipal (市定)	Original National Taiwan University College of Medicine【台大醫學院舊館】	1998.03.25	Zhong zheng（中正區）
40	Municipal (市定)	Taiwan Radio Broadcasting Station【台灣廣播電台放送亭】	1998.03.25	Zhong zheng（中正區）
41	Municipal (市定)	Taipei First Girls' High School【台北第一高女】	1998.03.25	Zhong zheng（中正區）
42	Municipal (市定)	Old Police Headquarter of Northern Precinct【原台北北警察署】	1998.03.25	Datong（大同區）
43	Municipal (市定)	Beitou Presbyterian Church【長老教會北投教堂】	1998.03.25	Beitou（北投區）
44	Municipal (市定)	Puji Temple of Beitou【北投普濟寺】	1998.03.25	Beitou（北投區）
45	Municipal (市定)	Old Taiwan Bank Dormitory【北投台灣銀行舊宿舍】	1998.03.25	Beitou（北投區）
46	Municipal (市定)	Grass Mountain Teachers' Training Center【草山教師研習中心】	1998.03.25	Beitou（北投區）
47	Municipal (市定)	Remains of Taipei Prison Wall【台北監獄圍牆遺跡】	1998.03.25	Daan（大安區）
48	Municipal (市定)	Original Building of Taihoku College【台灣師範大學原高等學校校舍】	1998.03.25	Daan（大安區）
49	Municipal (市定)	Original Building of Taihoku Imperial University【台灣大學原帝大校舍】	1998.03.25	Daan（大安區）
50	Municipal (市定)	Huguo Chan Buddhist Temple of the Linji School【臨濟護國禪寺】	1998.04.13	Zhongshan（中山區）
51	Municipal (市定)	The "Red Building," Chien-Kuo High School【建國中學紅樓】	1998.05.04	Zhong zheng（中正區）
52	Municipal (市定)	Japanese Colonial-era Taiwan Telegraph Bureau【台灣總督府交通局遞信部】	1998.05.04	Zhong zheng（中正區）
53	Municipal (市定)	Japanese Colonial-era Taipei Credit Cooperative【原台北信用組合】	1998.05.04	Zhong zheng（中正區）
54	Municipal (市定)	Residence of Taiwan Power Corporation Director【台灣電力株式會社社長宿舍】	1998.05.04	Zhong zheng（中正區）
55	Municipal (市定)	Taiwan Bank【台灣銀行】	1998.05.04	Zhong zheng（中正區）
56	Municipal (市定)	Japanese Colonial-era Imperial Life Insurance Building【帝國生命會社舊廈】	1998.05.04	Zhong zheng（中正區）
57	Municipal (市定)	Japanese Colonial-era Telephone Switching Office【台灣總督府電話交換局】	1998.05.04	Zhong zheng（中正區）
58	Municipal (市定)	Jinan Presbyterian Church【濟南基督長老教會】	1998.05.04	Zhong zheng（中正區）
59	Municipal (市定)	National Taiwan University College of Law【台大法學院】	1998.05.04	Zhong zheng（中正區）
60	Municipal (市定)	Old Taipei City Hall【台北市政府舊廈】	1998.05.04	Datong（大同區）
61	Municipal (市定)	Yinsong Pavilion【吟松閣】	1998.05.04	Beitou（北投區）
62	Municipal (市定)	The main gate of National Taiwan University【台灣大學校門】	1998.05.04	Daan（大安區）
63	Municipal (市定)	Old Taipei City Health Department【台北市政府衛生局舊址】	1998.05.04	Zhongshan（中山區）
64	Municipal (市定)	Neihu Qing Dynasty Quarry【內湖清代採石場】	1998.05.04	Neihu（內湖區）
65	National (國定)	Taiwan Monopoly Bureau Building【專賣局】	1998.06.10	Zhong zheng（中正區）
66	National (國定)	Taiwan Viceroy's Office Museum【台灣總督府博物館】	1998.06.10	Zhong zheng（中正區）
67	Municipal (市定)	Original Mitsui & Co. Building【三井物產株式會社舊廈】	1998.07.22	Zhong zheng（中正區）
68	Municipal (市定)	The "Red Building,"Taipei School of Industry【台北工業學校紅樓】	1998.07.22	Daan（大安區）

Number 序號	Class 級別	Name 標的物	Date 公告日	District 行政區
69	National（國定）	Presidential Office Building【總統府】	1998.07.30	Zhong zheng（中正區）
70	National（國定）	Control Yuan【監察院】	1998.07.30	Zhong zheng（中正區）
71	National（國定）	Executive Yuan【行政院】	1998.07.30	Zhong zheng（中正區）
72	National（國定）	Taipei Guest House【台北賓館】	1998.07.30	Zhong zheng（中正區）
73	National（國定）	Japanese Colonial-era High Court【司法大廈】	1998.07.30	Zhong zheng（中正區）
74	Municipal（市定）	Chinese Women's Anti-Aggression League Building【婦聯總會舊址】	1998.09.01	Zhong zheng（中正區）
75	Municipal（市定）	Former Japanese Military Hospital, Beitou Branch【前日軍衛戍醫院北投分院】	1998.09.01	Beitou（北投區）
76	Municipal（市定）	Grass Mountain Royal Guest House【草山御賓館】	1998.09.01	Shilin（士林區）
77	Municipal（市定）	Shilin Public Market【士林公有市場】	1998.09.01	Shilin（士林區）
78	Municipal（市定）	Taiwan Folk Arts Museum【北投文物館】	1998.09.01	Beitou（北投區）
79	Municipal（市定）	Dadaocheng Gu's Family Mansion【大稻埕辜宅】	1998.10.07	Datong（大同區）
80	Municipal（市定）	Beitou Grotto for the Buddhist Deity Acala【北投不動明王石窟】	1998.10.14	Beitou（北投區）
81	Municipal（市定）	Zhongshan Presbyterian Church【中山基督長老教會】	1998.10.14	Zhongshan（中山區）
82	Municipal（市定）	Yuanshan Villa【圓山別莊】	1998.10.14	Zhongshan（中山區）
83	Municipal（市定）	Manka Hsieh Family Residence【艋舺謝宅】	1999.01.07	Wanhua（萬華區）
84	Municipal（市定）	Lao-Song Elementary School【老松國小】	1999.06.29	Wanhua（萬華區）
85	Municipal（市定）	Taipei Grand Mosque【清真寺】	1999.06.29	Daan（大安區）
86	Municipal（市定）	Huang Family Qianrang Estate【龍安陂黃宅謙讓居】	1999.06.29	Daan（大安區）
87	Municipal（市定）	Fanglan Mansion【芳蘭大厝】	1999.06.29	Daan（大安區）
88	Municipal（市定）	Neihu Village Public Hall【內湖庄役場會議室】	1999.06.29	Neihu（內湖區）
89	Municipal（市定）	Guo Family Estate【內湖郭氏古宅】	1999.06.29	Neihu（內湖區）
90	Municipal（市定）	Tsai Jui-Yueh Dance Research Institute【蔡瑞月舞蹈研究社】	1999.12.31	Zhongshan（中山區）
91	Municipal（市定）	Tomb of Pan Gong-chou【潘宮籌墓】	1999.12.31	Shilin（士林區）
92	National（國定）	Yen Chia-kan's Residence【嚴家淦故居】	2000.04.27	Zhong zheng（中正區）
93	Municipal（市定）	Jianguo Beer Factory【建國啤酒廠】	2000.06.30	Zhongshan（中山區）
94	Municipal（市定）	Manka Lin Family Residence【艋舺林宅】	2000.07.11	Wanhua（萬華區）
95	Municipal（市定）	Ciyun Temple【慈雲寺】	2000.07.11	Wanhua（萬華區）
96	National（國定）	Official Residence of Chiang Kai-shek and Soong Mei-ling, Shilin【蔣中正宋美齡士林官邸】	2000.07.14	Shilin（士林區）
97	Municipal（市定）	Taiwan Railway Administration Taipei Railyard Bathhouse【鐵路局台北機廠澡堂】	2000.09.22	Xinyi（信義區）
98	Municipal（市定）	The Beitou Granary【北投穀倉】	2000.11.03	Beitou（北投區）
99	Municipal（市定）	Songshan Tabacco Plant【松山菸廠】	2001.09.28	Xinyi（信義區）
100	Municipal（市定）	Dadaocheng Presbyterian Church【台灣基督長老教會】	2002.05.28	Datong（大同區）
101	Municipal（市定）	Li Kuo-ting's Residence【李國鼎故居】	2003.01.20	Zhong zheng（中正區）
102	Municipal（市定）	Freedom House【自由之家】	2003.01.21	Zhong zheng（中正區）

Number 序號	Class 級別	Name 標的物	Date 公告日	District 行政區
103	Municipal (市定)	Taipei Brewery【台北酒廠】	2003.03.17	Zhong zheng (中正區)
104	Municipal (市定)	Unity House (including tennis courts)【大同之家】	2003.04.23	Zhong zheng (中正區)
105	Municipal (市定)	Dadaocheng Traffic Circle Air Defense Reservoir【大稻埕圓環防空蓄水池】	2003.09.23	Datong (大同區)
106	Municipal (市定)	Taiwan Sugar Company Taipei Warehouse【台糖台北倉庫】	2003.09.23	Wanhua (萬華區)
107	Municipal (市定)	Japanese Colonial-era Armed Forces Headquarters【原台灣軍司令部】	2004.01.15	Zhong zheng (中正區)
108	Municipal (市定)	Japanese Colonial-era Army Commander's Residence【原台灣軍司令官官邸】	2004.01.15	Zhong zheng (中正區)
109	Municipal (市定)	Yin Foo-sun's Residence【殷海光故居】	2004.02.09	Daan (大安區)
110	Municipal (市定)	Kishu An【紀州庵】	2004.02.12	Zhong zheng (中正區)
111	Municipal (市定)	Grass Mountain Waterworks【草山水道系統】	2004.04.28	Shilin、Beitou (士林區、北投區)
112	Municipal (市定)	Pan Family House, Shilin【士林潘宅】	2004.04.28	Shilin (士林區)
113	Municipal (市定)	Japanese Colonial-era housing for civil servants on Qidong Street【齊東街日氏宿舍】	2004.10.01	Zhong zheng (中正區)
114	Municipal (市定)	The Yen Hsi-shan House【閻錫山故居】	2004.10.07	Shilin (士林區)
115	Municipal (市定)	Manka Hong's Family Ancestral Shrine【艋舺洪氏祖厝】	2005.01.26	Wanhua (萬華區)
116	Municipal (市定)	The White House, Tianmu（Former U.S. Military Advisors Residence)【天母白屋】	2005.01.27	Shilin (士林區)
117	Municipal (市定)	The Zhong Shan Building, Yangmingshan【陽明山中山樓】	2005.04.26	Beitou (北投區)
118	Municipal (市定)	Dadaocheng Qianqiu Street Stores【大稻埕千秋街店屋】	2005.05.10	Datong (大同區)
119	Municipal (市定)	Tomb of Wang Deyi【王義德墓】	2006.01.10	Nangang (南港區)
120	Municipal (市定)	Nishi hongan Tample【西本願寺】	2006.02.21	Wanhua (萬華區)
121	Municipal (市定)	Songshan Market【松山市場】	2006.03.22	Songshan (松山區)
122	Municipal (市定)	Japanese Colonial-era Forestry Department Housing【總督府山林課宿舍】	2006.03.31	Daan (大安區)
123	Municipal (市定)	Sun Yun-suan's Residence, Chongqing South Road【孫運璿重慶南路寓所】	2006.06.23	Zhong zheng (中正區)
124	Municipal (市定)	Nanhai Academy Science Hall【南海學園科學館舊址】	2006.06.26	Zhong zheng (中正區)
125	Municipal (市定)	Manka General Zhushun Temple【艋舺助順將軍廟】	2006.07.05	Wanhua (萬華區)
126	Municipal (市定)	Xinfu Market【新富市場】	2006.07.05	Wanhua (萬華區)
127 (市定)	Municipal	Qihai House（Former Residence of President Chiang Ching-kuo)【七海寓所】	2006.07.18	Zhongshan (中山區)
128	Municipal (市定)	Japanese Colonial-era Residence, Nancai Garden District【前南菜園日式宿舍】	2006.07.25	Zhong zheng (中正區)
129	Municipal (市定)	National Taiwan University Japanese-style Housing – Ma Ting-ying Residence【國立台灣大學日式宿舍－馬廷英故居】	2006.11.01	Daan (大安區)
130	Municipal (市定)	National Taiwan University Japanese-style Housing – Wung Tung-ying Residence【國立台灣大學日式宿舍－翁通楹寓所】	2006.11.01	Daan (大安區)
131	Municipal (市定)	National Taiwan University Japanese-style Housing – Lo Tung-bin Residence【國立台灣大學日式宿舍－羅銅壁寓所】	2006.11.01	Daan (大安區)
132	Municipal (市定)	Chen Tian-Lai Residence【陳天來故居】	2006.12.15	Datong (大同區)
133	Municipal (市定)	Uen Meng Building on Guisui Street【歸綏街文萌樓】	2006.12.15	Datong (大同區)

國家圖書館出版品預行編目資料

Historical Sites in Taipei I :
The Most Updated Directory of 133 Historical Sites in Taipei
台北市古蹟巡覽 上冊：最新版台北133座古蹟中英文簡介
-- 初版 . -- 台北市：藝術家出版社 , 2007〔民96〕
160面；14×22公分. --中英對照
ISBN　978-986-7034-35-9（上冊：平裝）
1. 台北市 — 古蹟

673.29/101.6　　　　　　　　　　　　　95026632

Historical Sites in Taipei　I
台 北 市 古 蹟 巡 覽 上冊

Curator: Department of Cultural Affairs,Taipei City Government,
and Artist Publishing Co.
策劃 / 台北市文化局、藝術家出版社
Editor: Artist Publishing Co.
編輯出版 / 藝術家出版社

發行人　何政廣
主編　王庭玫
中文解說　台北市文化局・藝術家出版社
英文翻譯　台北市文化局、黃敏裕、謝汝萱

圖片提供　台北市文化局、藝術家出版社
文字編輯　謝汝萱、王雅玲
地圖編輯　周佩璇
美術設計　曾小芬

出版者　藝術家出版社
地址　台北市重慶南路一段147號6樓
電話（02）2371-9692～3／傳真（02）2331-7096
郵政劃撥　01044798 藝術家雜誌社帳戶

總經銷　時報文化出版企業股份有限公司
倉庫　台北縣中和市連城路134巷16號
電話　（02）2306-6842
郵政劃撥　00176200 帳戶

南部區域代理　台南市西門路一段223巷10弄26號
電話（06）261-7268／傳真（06）263-7698

製版印刷　欣佑彩色製版印刷股份有限公司
初版　2007年1月
定價　新台幣200元

ISBN　978-986-7034-35-9 （平裝）